For Love of A Dog

Jenny Desoutter

With illustrations by the author

Published by Skipper Publications

April 2015

ISBN 978-0-9568571-2-5

Copyright © Jenny Desoutter 2015

skipperpublications@gmail.com
Printed in Cornwall by TJ International Ltd

In memory of my mother, Dorothy, who loved all living creatures, especially dogs and horses; and also of Paddy, her first dog, and Tansy, her second.

Preface

Bobbin was my first dog, and he changed my life.

Through him, I learnt so much that is important - to look, to listen, to value the moment, and to live life to the full every day. His companionship not only meant that I was never alone and always felt safe, but also opened up to me whole new dimensions, wherever we were, whatever we were doing, and whoever we were with.

What I learnt through the time I spent with him is nothing new, nothing extraordinary. It is only what everyone who has a dog companion knows and understands very well. But for me it was a revelation and a constant delight which transformed not only every moment, but also my understanding of life.

It was the joy that I found in his companionship, and above all in the vitality, innocence and freshness of his approach to life, that prompted me to record in these pages what is nothing unusual, and yet something very precious: the enrichment and happiness that the friendship of a dog can bring, if only we have the time and good fortune to know it.

This memoir was written in 1997, when Bobbin was fourteen. He lived, still enjoying life, until he was eighteen. The lessons that he taught me - continued now by Skipper - are still enriching mine.

Jenny Desoutter
Dorking, 2015

Contents

Chapter One	The Start of it All	1
Chapter Two	Coming Home	5
Chapter Three	Early Days	9
Chapter Four	Growing Up	14
Chapter Five	Working Together	21
Chapter Six	Building a Relationship	30
Chapter Seven	A Little Faith in My Friends	37
Chapter Eight	Meeting Other Dogs	45
Chapter Nine	A Dog's Senses	53
Chapter Ten	Meetings By the Way	61
Chapter Eleven	Rabbits and Squirrels: Fair Game	69
Chapter Twelve	Best Friends	77
Chapter Thirteen	A Friend in Need	86
Chapter Fourteen	Travelling Dog	95
Chapter Fifteen	Not So Tough Dog	104
Chapter Sixteen	Visits to the Vet	111
Chapter Seventeen	Understanding Each Other	119
Chapter Eighteen	These Humans!	130
Chapter Nineteen	Growing Older	141
Chapter Twenty	The Very Best Friend of All	149

For Love of a Dog

Chapter 1: The Start Of It All

I don't really know what it was, one dank November evening almost fifteen years ago, that made me suddenly think, "I want a dog."

It had been many years since Tansy, our Welsh Springer Spaniel, had been an important part of the family when I was a child. But I had not, until now, thought of getting a dog of my own. Perhaps it had gone through my mind at some vague level where millions of possibilities drift in and out of the lower levels of consciousness, but if so, I don't remember. All I can recall is the sudden overwhelming desire to get a puppy - and to get it *now*; and I knew, too, what sort of puppy I wanted. It was to be a Jack Russell.

It was half past four in the afternoon, but it might just as well have been the middle of the night. Outside, the thick ugly fog had barely lifted the hem of its smothering skirts all day; now it had congealed itself into an impenetrable light-choking darkness. Beyond the blank window there was no sign of the garden.

But just as this recognition of an undeniable desire had come suddenly, so too it came with an urgency and a sense of purpose that would brook no delay. I wanted a dog: I would go and find one now. I didn't think of looking in the paper, or of asking in pet shops or at the vet's, or any of the usual ways one might plan to look for a dog. But then I didn't really stop to think at all. I just knew that I must have a dog; and I searched frantically through the archives of my gathering brain for the next clue.

Then in a flash I remembered: clear in my mind, I suddenly saw a sign I had noticed stuck up outside a house a year or two before, "Jack Russell puppies for sale. Apply within." I wasn't exactly sure which house it was, but I was sure enough that it was on the outskirts of Billingshurst - about half an hour's drive away, on a good day.

I knew it was unwise to go out on what was really an unnecessary journey on this sort of evening. But I couldn't wait. Within a few minutes I was in the car and heading southwards. If I had stopped to

For Love of a Dog

think at all rationally, I would have realised that it was verging on the insane to drive twenty miles looking for puppies which would have been sold over a year ago. But then, I didn't stop to think for a moment.

I don't remember how long the journey took; it must have been the best part of an hour. All I remember is the heavy grey pall of sodden fog that blocked all the world from my eyes except for the tiny space in front of the car which revealed itself grudgingly a few feet at a time. I felt isolated and tired, rolled in this desolate blanket, and my eyes ached. I wished now that I had thought to have a cup of tea, or bring a sandwich; but tired and hungry as I was, I never once thought of turning back. The certainty which had descended into my consciousness burned brightly and steadily in my mind: the vision of a little Jack Russell would not be pushed away. My only anxiety was that I should get there quickly enough; for some incomprehensible reason I had a fear of being too late.

I vaguely remember the woman's gaze of amazement when she opened the door and I explained why I had come. Yes, she said, she had had some puppies for sale last year, but her bitch wouldn't be having any more. She must have caught the sense of urgency which had brought me there, for although she clearly had some reservations about the state of mind of someone who had selected such an evening to drive round the countryside looking for dogs, she invited me in out of the dripping gloom and sat me down with a cup of tea while she had a think. But no, she didn't think she knew anyone else who might have any puppies right now - she thought a friend was going to breed in the spring, if I could wait. I couldn't.

I got up to go, feeling suddenly even more tired and for the first time wondering what on earth had possessed me to come all this way on such an errand, and whether I would be able to get home safely in the blinding dark of the fog, or whether this was some cruel ploy of fate to trick me into a pointless catastrophe on an invisible road on a night unfit for man or beast to be abroad. I heaved a sigh and switched on the ignition. Suddenly the kitchen door opened again.

"I've just had a thought: you could try Mrs. Carslake over at Epsom. They've got Jack Russells, and I know she said she might have pups one day. I think this is her phone number...." and she pressed into my hand a scrap of paper which was to change my life.

It was too late when I got home to go over to Epsom: the Carslakes were going out. But that night I could hardly sleep for knowing that tomorrow afternoon I would be seeing not one, but two litters of puppies.
"The two of them whelped within a few days of each other. We thought it would be easier like that. Titch is the mother, it's her third litter, but it's Sally's first. No, no one has been to see them yet - we've just put an advert in the paper and it doesn't come out till tomorrow."
The puppies were just six weeks old today.
"They're all lovely, but one of them is a proper little Christian; it's got the nicest temperament of any pup I've ever come across .... but I won't tell you which it is, you'll have to make up your own mind. You'll know which one is for you."

And she was absolutely right. The Carslakes' house was small, and it had been entirely taken over by ten squirming, piddling little concentrations of will the size of small rats. I sat on the sofa and watched them; they moved so fast and unpredictably, and their teeth were so sharp I almost felt as if I were besieged by rats. I wanted a bitch, so Mrs. Carslake picked out the girls and handed each of them to me in turn. Some bit me with a ferocity that I felt was completely uncalled-for; only one took my eye. But try as I might, she would not stay on my lap. Her one desire was to get away and back to her wriggling, nipping siblings. The other bitches seemed even less attractive, and even more antagonistic.

Then, suddenly, I saw him: soft and floppy and black and white and tan, and somehow quieter than the rest and a little aloof. Down the centre of his face was a dividing line - dark one side and white the other, and he looked up at me with eyes like pools and as black as ink. For a long moment he held my eyes; then slowly, but surely, and with a few little wobbles, he padded over the scuffled newspaper towards me and sat at my feet gazing up with a look I shall never forget. It was a look of certainty and trust.

The others had melted away into the background now; they were nothing to me, and I was clearly nothing to them. There was only one dog in that room, and he was sitting quietly on my lap, every now and then giving me a little tentative lick. I put him down with the others. He turned round at once and came back to me. Again I put him back with the others, and picked up the bitch puppy once more. As fast as she struggled and nipped me, he was back at my feet with a reproachful look even faster. And there he stayed.

Or rather there we both would have stayed, gazing at each other, if Mrs. Carslake hadn't hinted that her husband would be wanting his tea, and would I collect him Saturday if I had made up my mind.
"But he'll hardly be seven weeks old! Surely that's too young .... "
But with ten growing, squabbling, biting puppies in the house I could see her point of view.
"He'll be all right," she said.

Chapter 2: Coming Home

And he was.

I don't know how he spent the next four days - looking forward to a good night's sleep, I expect. But for me they were frantic.

I was working full time, and with Christmas only three weeks away I was even busier than usual. So unplanned had been my decision to get a dog, that I had given almost no thought to what he might need. But I managed to talk Harry, the kindly caretaker, into making a "bodged-up" wooden box in which the puppy could sleep and travel. It had at least occurred to me that he would need some kind of restraint in the car if we were both to be safe. I looked out some old jumpers and a stone hot water bottle, and a good friend started knitting a couple of blankets. I cleared a space in the kitchen for his box bed: and that was all the preparation he got. I hope I have made up for any hastiness since.

When I went to Epsom the next Saturday, the fourth of December, to collect him, I little realised what I was taking on. I knew I was getting a dog, which would be fun, and that he would keep me company and come out riding with me and my pony. I knew I should grow fond of him, and that I would need to look after him, and keep him healthy. But no experience I had ever had could have prepared me for the way he would, surely and steadily, just as he had first approached me, take over the whole of my life. I knew nothing of how he would adopt me into his pack, and find ways of protecting me when he could, and only occasionally look to me for reassurance. I could not then know how his fears would become my fears, and how my anxieties would be reflected in his dejected demeanour; how he would help me to distinguish friend from foe, or how he would teach me to look through his eyes, and to see everything around me with a new perspective which I would little by little begin to understand; or how he would in the end dictate as surely as if he could speak what we should do each day, and where we should go. I had no idea how the phrase 'man's best friend' could really mean *best* beyond all comparison.

For Love of a Dog

He lies next to me now, stretched on the spare bed, enjoying the last of the evening sun. He has had a sore paw the last two or three days, and it is wrapped up in a sock. There is a sound of blissful snoring, and his eyes flicker occasionally as the vision of a rabbit - perhaps not quite escaping - flits through his dreaming brain.

A lot of rabbits have got away from him since that chilly December day when he left his squirming, squeaking, sharp-toothed nest of brothers and sisters and was carried out into the future, wrapped in a shawl and cosied by a stone hot water bottle: you might say, without a backward look. Snuggled warmly in his wooden box on the passenger seat, he seemed already to know that he was where he should be, completely in control, and apparently perfectly contented. Looking about him with an air of polite curiosity, he swayed and wobbled with the movement of the car, and then settled down to sleep as though all were as it should be. He was going home.

From the start, he was a model puppy. Although I had only a little experience of puppy training, and that little so long ago it was almost forgotten, I hardly needed any. He on the other hand, seemed to have no hesitancy or doubts about training me: a process which continues to this day. After his meals of minced-up ox heart and puppy meal, I popped him outside the back door for a few moments, or wandered slowly down the path, followed by a padding roly-poly less than six inches high. Although his first six weeks had been spent in a muddle of newspapers drenched with the puddly smells of his brothers and sisters, he knew instinctively that this was different. Only once do I remember coming home to find an apologetic little puddle near the back door, and a shamefaced and forlorn greeting. For the rest, it was as if he were saying, "House training? Who needs house training?"

Any other anxieties I had had, he dealt with in a similar way. It was as if he had listened in to the head-shaking words of warning that well-meaning friends had felt duty-bound to deliver in the few days before his arrival, no doubt rightly thinking that such a sudden decision could not have been thoroughly thought through. What would happen while I was at work? And Jack Russells were supposed to be rather nippy and yappy - how would I manage if he bit the children, or howled the house down while I was out? And what if he was going to be car-sick every time we went out anywhere for the day? "Well, of course," I'd said airily, " He'll have to be all right in the car; it's no good if he's going to be car-sick. And it won't do if he howls all the time while I'm out - and he's got to be good with children or it simply won't work."

Within the first forty-eight hours he had set my mind at rest on all these points. In fact, as I say, he was the model puppy. Naturally, being a dog, he was to sleep downstairs, in the kitchen, in his wooden box. So on the first night, I tucked him in with his hot water bottle in case he should miss the warmth of his mother, and went up to bed rather early, convinced that I should get little sleep. But I would be firm; no amount of crying, however piteous, would induce me to go downstairs to him. That would be setting a hopeless precedent. He would, in the end, give up and fall asleep exhausted, having learnt that crying does no good. This was especially important as the following day I would have to leave him when I went to work: a moment I was dreading.

I lay upstairs and waited .... and waited .... until I suppose I must eventually have fallen asleep. There was never a sound - not even a tiny squeak. When I awoke the next morning, there was still no sound and I rushed downstairs convinced that a dreadful disaster had befallen him. I was greeted by a thumping little tail, and a sleepy yawn from a very cosy little dog stretched comfortably in his box. He scrambled out, and I put him in the garden and then gave him his breakfast. When I went back upstairs to get dressed, he whimpered plaintively for a few minutes; and when he was quiet, I went back downstairs. And that was the only time he ever cried at being left.

But of course the big test was to come on Monday, when I would have to go to work, and leave him on his own. Fortunately, the school where I was working at that time was just a two minute walk down the road, and I would only have to leave him from nine o'clock until lunchtime at twelve. I would hare back up the road, using the car to gain a few seconds; and then he would have to be on his own again from one fifteen until three thirty. Although he had been so good at night-time, I was naturally worried that this might prove just too distressing for him - to be left so long on his own when he must still be missing his Mum and his family. So I arranged for a friend to come and listen outside the door every half hour, and at any rate to go in and check up at eleven o'clock.

For Love of a Dog

I think she was as amazed as I had been. Having heard no sounds of any sort from inside the house, she finally crept in and saw - a tiny puppy curled up and soundly asleep in his bed. He looked up rather dozily as if to say,
"Well? Haven't you got anything better to do? Very pleased to meet you, I'm sure, but now perhaps you'll let me get on with my sleeping. I've got a lot of growing to do."

Needless to say, when he met the children, he seemed not only to revel in the attention, but also to love each and every one of them as if he knew how special a puppy dog is to five-year-olds, and it was his mission in life to bring an extra bit of love to anyone who needed it. As Mrs. Carslake would have said, "He's a proper little Christian."

Or maybe it was because he came into our lives when the spirit of Christmas was abroad: the best Christmas present I could ever have had.

Chapter 3: Early Days

It was surprisingly difficult to think of a name for him; and it wasn't made any easier by the fact that there are no limits on possible names for dogs. I must have run through hundreds in my mind before he found his very own name. In the earliest days, he was so soft and cuddly that he somehow acquired the name of Fudge. I did wonder whether this might be rejected when he grew older, as being rather whimsical and undignified, but in fact the name stuck for two or three months - and I have one friend from that time who still takes me by surprise, asking "And how is Fudge?"

As he became sturdier and more assertive, he began to outgrow his baby name, and feeling rather like Turandot, I began the search all over again. Crumble, Crumpet, Nebuchadnezzar, Georgie, Benjamin.... I would whisper the names softly as he lay curled up on his cushion, seeking inspiration from his latest exploit, or a trick of the light; or I would try calling him when he was sniffing something interesting under a hedge, or busy chewing an old sock. But he answered to none of these, and I must say I couldn't blame him, as they quite obviously did not fit. It was beginning to seem as if he might live his life as The Dog With a Different Name Every Week, unless I could come up with something soon.

But of course, it all fell into place when the time was right. He must have been three or four months old by the time I eventually discovered his name. We were going for a walk one afternoon, and he was running along in front of me on a grassy path near our field. I looked at his small compact figure bouncing along, doing an odd little rock from back to front feet and keeping up a cheerful jogging pace - just as I was to watch him so many times in years to come - ears flapping, tail up, knees scarcely bending, nose concentrating on the task in hand. Then suddenly, without any warning, a voice from inside me called out, "Bobbin!" and straight away, as if I had at last touched the right switch, he stopped and put his head on one side and listened with all his attention. Then he turned round, and with a happy bounce he bobbed back towards me. It was as though he had been waiting for that name all his short life. At any rate, he recognised it at once: and so did I.

Those early days were a joyous time of adventure and discovery for both of us. They were days of close watching and listening: he alert to everything that I did or said, striving to learn the meanings in a gesture, a word, a glance. I, on the other hand, was continually enchanted by the antics of this winsome, flirtatious bundle of adventurousness and affection, who attacked and welcomed the world with enthusiastic gusts of energy, followed by sudden collapses and blissful sleeps.

Bobbin fitted so naturally into my life that it was hardly necessary to make any adjustments. He very quickly came to understand the pattern of my days by which the pattern of his days too must be ordered. Breakfast at half past seven, and a little wander in the garden. I would leave for work at half past eight, and he would curl up and sleep till I came home at midday. In fact, he soon realised that interrupting his slumbers for a lunch break was scarcely worthwhile, and after the very early months he didn't even bother to stir when I rushed home to let him out at lunchtime. He knew I was in a hurry - it was hardly worth getting out of bed; better to save his energies until four o'clock when our day could really start.

But to say there had to be few adjustments is not to say that he did not make a difference. With eyes of innocence he greeted the world, and was spurred on by the boundless curiosity which is natural to youth. Every object he encountered had to be investigated and tested, every new place was an adventure, every new friend a blessing to be leapt over and adored. I found myself, with an unforeseen sense of discovery, beginning to see the world from a totally new perspective, discovering, with this self-possessed bundle of puppyhood, dangers and excitements I had never imagined before.

He welcomed everything and everyone he encountered with unstinting passion, and many a friend of mine reeled from the impact of his projectile enthusiasm with punctured knees or bruised thighs. Yet with that sixth sense that seems so often to inform a dog's behaviour, he instinctively knew the difference between child and adult, and he was always careful not to jump up at a child - unless, of course, they were holding a tempting toy and were obviously inviting him to play a game.

And oh! What games he played! From his little platefuls of meat and biscuit what an unending store of energy he derived! Wherever we were, he would find something to toss and throw and chase. Socks and cushions, fir cones and dusters, all were cast pell-mell around the house, while in the garden he would worry and worry at a plant pot or a ball of baler twine. His inventiveness was fascinating to observe, and when we were on a walk I began to revel with him in his excitement, or to smile in anticipation if I saw a scrap of black fertiliser bag ahead of us on the path. He was, of course, simply following generations of genetically stored hunting instincts; he was practising how to stalk, sprint, pounce, and finally shake and shake the life out of the hapless plastic, whilst terrifying it with ferocious growls. But the unmistakable joy with which he tackled every new challenge became for me a constantly renewable source of inspiration.

The infectious vitality of his movements, and the laughter in his eyes never failed to grip my attention; it was as if through him I could enjoy the carefree zest of puppyhood, too. I wanted to join in, to be one of his pack; and I tried hard to teach him to give up his plaything, so that we could share the game, and enjoy that traditional man-and-dog version of throw and catch. But the idea of letting go of something once he had captured it seemed to be abhorrent to his most deeply rooted instincts: removing a prize from his mouth could be a risky business, and I had to give up the attempt. This was obviously one game that Bobbin had no intention of playing.

Every walk was an adventure; and one of his greatest thrills was to encounter, in an otherwise dull and empty field, a tussock of grass. Suddenly, he would spot a clump which was robuster than the rest, standing out in lumpish profile amid the waving forest of green. At once he would freeze, one ear pricked, and then with a cannoning rush he would charge, seize his prey, and try to kill it. You might think this would be easily done; but no, capture was one thing, certain victory another. Observing it closely lest it escape while his teeth were for a moment withdrawn, he would challenge it with chilling barks, as if urging it at least to try to put up some sort of a fight. When his taunting failed to produce a response, he would employ a more vigorous method, backing off and racing round and round the defeatist tussock, making occasional sallies at it, and rolling his eyes threateningly. Then, just as suddenly, he would apparently lose all interest in it, and race off on another quest. I think he might have joined King Arthur's round table - or maybe he was re-living the adventures of Sancho Panza.

But the day that stands out in my memory for sheer fun, was the first time we went to the seaside. Although in later life he has found the beach lacking in good quality smells, and also hard on his feet, that first time at Lyme Regis was like coming to a puppies' paradise.

It was winter time, and the beach was empty: empty of people, that is, but for Bobbin it was full of unimaginable treasures. Bobbin looked with amazement at the sea; it didn't stay still, so it must be alive. He tried to chase it, barking and skipping in alarm each time the outgoing wave changed its mind and turned round after him. Then he found that at least he could have some fun snatching away its toys, and again and again he ran into the edge of the brine and emerged triumphant with a long trail of rope, or a chunk of seaweed, or a plastic bottle.

What fun he had with the plastic bottles! He would chase and chase them as they rolled bumpily over the pebbles, exulting in the strange groans they emitted when he pinned them to the ground. Then in a gust of wind, off they would go again, defiant down the beach, and the game would begin once more. We spent hours on the beach that day, my usual search for fossils quite abandoned, as well it should be, in favour of the thrill of discovery and sheer fun that I was privileged to share in.

And so through those early days of our friendship, Bobbin began to reveal the strands of his nature that would mark his life and mine with gifts of joy and wonder: his fearlessness, his quick sympathy for the mood of those around him, and his capacity for vivacity and fun. As each day passed, the podgy puppy who had weighed no more than a bag of sugar when he made his first journey into the unknown, grew a little more into an adventurous young dog, and began, not so much to fit into my way of life, as to lead me towards a partnership in his.

Chapter 4: Growing Up

The fun that we shared in those early days seemed to go on and on. Although when he slept, he slept soundly, when he was awake Bobbin's energy and enthusiasm seemed to be inexhaustible. In anything and everything that he encountered, Bobbin saw, with that unerring instinct of the healthy puppy, yet another opportunity for a game. I thought of doing the washing-up: he would not be satisfied until he had the dishcloth in his teeth. I decided to vacuum the carpet: Bobbin would be there every inch of the floor, just in front of the hoover, as if he were marking an opponent in a game of football. I had to empty the washing machine - catching the clothes as they came out was a wonderful game. Or perhaps he thought he was helping ....

Gradually I came to realise that from now on he would be a part of *everything* I did - and not necessarily play the part that I might have imagined I would prefer. He was always careful: however active his participation, he somehow contrived to be so gentle that he never damaged anything that was of any importance. Nevertheless, I have to admit that there were times when I, in my comparative old age, found his exuberance and ebullience a stringent test of my imperfect patience - times when I wished he would just sit down and be quiet!

When I came home from work, I was temporarily drained of energy; but of course, in Bobbin's eyes, this was the real start of his day's activity - the time he had been waiting for, when the fun could begin, and he could start to use up some of the energy he had been storing during his day-long sleep. Before I had time to get my breath, he was ready for a game of "See if you can get your hairbrush back!" All I wanted was to sit down for a few moments' peace and have a cup of tea, but I found instead I was racing up and down the garden battling for the floor mop or a wellington boot.

This, of course, is an eternal dilemma: the incompatibility of youth and age, the crux of the generation gap. It is a syndrome that any parent of young children will recognise, and it can never, for our own good, be fully resolved. Too late we realise it is a time to be treasured.

When Bobbin was just a year old, we moved house. For a few weeks there were builders coming and going; and for Bobbin this was a time of endless opportunity. Motivated - as he still is today - by a consuming desire to join in and be part of whatever is going on, Bobbin took a keen and vigilant interest in everything the workmen did. If there was sweeping up to be done, within a few moments Bobbin would have seized the dustpan or brush and chased with it down the garden. If a sheet of polythene was put down to catch the dust, Bobbin would be away with it as soon as our backs were turned. We humans had no choice but to accept Bobbin's terms and play the game. Only after we had pursued him, and he had had his fun, could what we considered the serious work continue.

On one occasion, the memory of which still fills me with a mixture of amusement and horror, Bobbin suddenly burst in from the garden covered from nose to tail in a strange pink dust. Between his teeth he bore triumphantly an empty paper sack. Hurrying to investigate, I discovered that he had been savaging the builder's bag of powdered plaster. Appalling visions went through my mind: what if it rained? I recollected a play we had once done at school called *"Passion, Poison and Petrifaction"*. Bobbin would become a statue of a dog, unable to move, and set forever in a rigid cast. Should I hope that a vigorous brushing would remove all the dust, or would it be better to take the bull by the horns and give him a thorough bath at once?

While I pondered this perplexing problem, the good-tempered builder looked on in amusement. His most stalwart and persevering attempts at carrying out a professional job had been interrupted time and again, and thwarted in a dozen different ways. Yet instead of becoming angry or impatient, he just looked at us both with a resigned expression of kindly tolerance. With a slow smile he commented,

"He does like a game, doesn't he?"

I must have muttered something apologetic about a bad dog, and how infuriating it was, because after a little pause he spoke some words which I have never forgotten:

" Yes, but you'll be sorry when he doesn't want to play any more!"

How true those words were! And spoken at that time when I was feeling most exasperated, they illuminated for me a new understanding of what it is to share one's life with a dog. I knew of course that he was right: that Bobbin's playfulness could not last forever; the time would come - all too soon - when he would no longer have that peculiar zest for life, and that irrepressible energy: and I knew that I should indeed be sorry. Suddenly, with a new poignancy, I realised that Bobbin's vivacity, though it might at times test my patience, was a priceless gift to be treasured and enjoyed.

From time to time since then, I have watched to see if he still wants to play a game. Of course, as the years have gone by, his enthusiasms have, little by little, almost imperceptibly diminished. His eagerness for games comes more rarely now, and is more fleeting. But what a rush of joy it brings me when he is suddenly, even now, seized by an impulse to have a tussle with my shoe; or when, infuriated by the attention I am giving to someone else, he makes a sudden attack on my handbag.

I have been grateful for those words. From that day on, my appreciation of Bobbin's right to his own individual life took on a new dimension. I began in that moment to understand that his whole perspective on life, though different from mine, was no less valid. I had been concerned that he should understand and fit in with my way of life: but in that moment I saw that it was no less important that I, too, should seek to see the world from his point of view. It was not good enough to dismiss his ventures into hilarity simply because his views of what is important don't happen to coincide with my own, or because he feels playful at an inconvenient moment. Perhaps, indeed, he has a right to challenge my set of values; and perhaps, too, I have something to learn from his innocent view of the world. I realised that my responsibility for his welfare also includes allowing him to be free to be happy in his own canine way, and I resolved to do all I could to ensure that every moment of his precious life would be just as good, in his terms, as it could be.

And how enriching it has been, to try to see through his eyes: and to perceive how flawed, from his simple and honest perspective, are many of the values I had previously taken for granted! Some friends find this attitude hard to understand; and there are some dog owners who appear to think that the whole point of having a dog is to be able to make it do only what you want it to do. But then history has shown that there have always been some who think the same about women, or children, or slaves, or employees. It doesn't mean that they are right.

Once, on a walk to the top of the North Downs, Bobbin found a ball. We had climbed up to the top of the hill so that I could study the orchids, and do some sketches of the view over the Dorking Gap. But when we were at the top, and I was busily making notes, Bobbin suddenly dived into the undergrowth and emerged carrying a large pink baby's ball. It was so large that, as he carried it triumphantly between his teeth, it almost obscured his shining eyes. It was made of thick plastic, and had letters of the alphabet embossed on it: and, joy of joys, it *squeaked*.

Like so many of his species, Bobbin has always had a consuming passion for squeaky toys: although usually his Jack Russell teeth defeat the squeak within about three minutes. But this ball was of a stouter plastic, and its squeak was made of sterner stuff. Bobbin's expressions of ecstasy at finding this treasure, and the fun we had as we chased it round and round on the top of the hill, were moments of a joy that was as sudden and unexpected as it has been unforgettable.

I have no recollection now about the orchids I found on that walk, or of the sketches: after all, I have studied orchids for dozens of years. But only once have we ever found a pink ball. All I remember is the grass and the sky, and the chasing and racing over and over again after the pink ball, until we could chase and race no more.

The discovery of that abandoned pink ball touched the day, and the place, with an exhilaration which will never be repeated. I carried it home, and although it still lies under the hedge in the garden, somehow its appeal has never returned. It was just a moment, touched with a special magic.

Now that he is older, there are fewer excitements in Bobbin's life. I suppose that, as for the rest of us, life holds fewer surprises. Where once there was novelty and intrigue, now there is familiarity and understanding. The sense of adventure has been overlaid with experience; predictability has come to outweigh possibility; there seem to be fewer mysteries in the world now to be discovered. And there is less energy with which to pursue them.

But there is still one enchantment that has never yet failed to excite: for Bobbin, Christmas has always held as much thrilling sense of expectancy and fun as it does for a five-year-old child. Perhaps it has memories for him of that first Christmas which he shared so soon after he came home; perhaps he is happy because it is a time when all the family are together, and he realises that this is a time which is different, and special. At any rate, there is no way that he is going to be left out.

From the first moment when he sets eyes on the Christmas tree, set like an island amid a sea of ribboned presents that overflow higgledy piggledy from the table on to the floor, his eyes shine with a bubbling ecstasy that I, for one, wish I could recapture. Up and down he races on the polished floor, slithering drunkenly in his eagerness to begin. After every two or three slides he stops, and begins urgently with his nose to sort out the muffled scents of the parcels, finding out secrets that none of the rest of us can know.

Of course he knows that he must wait until Christmas morning: he is not an unruly dog. But once he sees the first person go to collect a parcel from the tree, he cannot contain his excitement any longer. For then the fun can begin, and Bobbin knows that he can take part in it all.

Among all the piles of parcels there are, of course, several with Bobbin's name on; but his enjoyment is not motivated by personal greed. Chocolate drops and meaty chews are very welcome: but he is just as excited if he rips the paper off a scarf or a bottle of perfume: his all-embracing delight is a lesson to us all. As soon as one parcel is opened and admired, Bobbin is back at the tree rummaging around to see which one we should open next.

For Love of a Dog

He isn't interested in opening them by himself - he always waits until he has (with a little judicious assistance and advice) delivered them to the proper recipient. But then, with his paws up on their knees, he throws all his energy and skill into helping them do what he obviously thinks must be the whole point of the occasion: tearing off the paper. It must seem very strange to him. Why in the world should we all decide, once a year, to wrap anything and everything from tea towels to bedroom slippers in layers of paper, only to take them all off again and throw them away?

I hope we don't ever have a Christmas guest who takes a stuffy and possessive line about the proper role of a dog in the business of opening presents. The truth is that Bobbin seems to derive far greater pleasure from the process than anyone else. And unless one is feeling more than usually Scrooge-like about preserving the wrapping paper for another year, the sight of his shining eyes and wagging tail is worth more than all the jumpers and chocolates and talcum powder put together. His spontaneous enthusiasm infects us all with an inspiring spirit of seasonal joy, and his innocent delight does more than anything else to make Christmas day just as it should be: a day for laughter, and for sharing.

Chapter 5: Working Together

Christmas must seem very strange to Bobbin. But then, being the only dog in a household of humans is altogether an odd and unnatural existence for a dog. I often ask myself how I would cope if I were kept as a human pet in a world of, for example, elephants.

We have spent centuries in genetically adapting the canine species to suit our purposes; but still, fortunately, we have not in any way diminished the fundamental instincts which determine a dog's behaviour. And one of the most basic of these instincts is his desire to belong to a pack. However much a family pet may become 'domesticated', and taught to follow the customs desirable in his human family, he is able to do so just because he is by nature a pack animal, and because he needs above all else to belong, to be accepted, and to have his own place in his own special group. It is this very aspect of his nature which makes a dog so amenable to human society, and so willing to oblige his colleagues - or, as some would prefer to say, his master.

In order to be able to function as a pack member, a dog - just like the human pack members - must understand the language of his peers: he must be able to recognise and communicate warnings and signals of danger, and to work as part of a team; he must be able to sense the mood of others around him, and understand his own special role in the group. In this he does not differ appreciably from most human beings. But a dog living in a human pack has to exercise all his intelligence: for he must become proficient not only in dog language, but also in human communication. In effect, a family pet has to become bilingual.

But then, a household pet has plenty of time for his studies. After all, what else has he to do? If he were living in the wild, his life would be devoted to making provision for his basic needs. Working with others of his team, his chief task would be to sniff out some hapless prey, pursue, kill, and devour it. At times, he might have to fight over who should get the biggest share: and then he would sleep. Apart from hunting for food and sleeping, his time would perhaps be spent in some mutual grooming, some sparring with the youngsters, and when the time is right, courting and contesting over a mate. Life would be demanding and challenging, using every skill for the purpose of survival

A dog living among humans does not have the opportunity for any of these natural pursuits. He is not normally required to hunt for his tin of Doggovite; mating is usually off the agenda for most of the time - and in fact life could become boring to a degree.

Meanwhile, his human friends spend their time rushing around doing things which must seem totally pointless and incomprehensible to the household's canine contingent. But, content in the knowledge that his needs are fully provided for, and with long stretches of free time at his disposal, a dog of an inquiring turn of mind has ample opportunity to apply his mental energies to a lifetime's silent study of Human Behaviour. By simply observing, by using his highly-developed senses, and by exercising his excellent powers of memory, he can specialise in the interpretation of What Humans Do When, How To Know What They Are Going to Do, and How to Make the Most of the Services They Provide. Some dogs specialise in How to Make Them Feel Guilty with One Miserable Look; all develop their own special skills, once they have mastered the fundamentals. And as all owners know, they soon understand every word you say.

Dogs, like children, are very quick and eager learners. If we want our canine friend to achieve his full potential as an integrated member of our pack, we must make sure that he learns early on those things that we would like him to know. It is all very well having fun with a puppy, but the fun will soon turn sour unless a basic system of communication, and some ground rules for behaviour are clearly established. Just like the rest of us, a dog needs to know what is expected of him: and the more help we can give him in understanding his role in the household, the happier he (and his human friends) will be.

Bobbin's education began on his very first day. Although his formal training inevitably involved an element of discipline, this time of learning became also a precious time, and a time for great fun. Bobbin was very interested and appreciative when I clearly had something important to say just to him. He was like any child showing off his gold stars when he was able to demonstrate that he understood. This was a time of building up trust as well as communication, a time for exploring and deepening our relationship.

Humans, unlike dogs, most frequently prefer to communicate using words. Therefore, the early training of a dog is usually centred around the linking of specific command words with required behavioural responses.

Bobbin's first lesson was "Sit!" and he had no trouble at all in understanding what he was expected to do. I remember even now the expression of shining pride in his big eyes as he happily played this game over and over again. But not everything was so easy. The command "Stay!" proved considerably more baffling; and learning to obey was a severe challenge both to his inclinations and to the picture he had begun to build of his world. While he very quickly understood what he was required to do in theory, in practice his uplifted ears and anxious eyes conveyed with heart-rending poignancy his puzzlement and fear that I apparently wanted to leave him and go off by myself.

This was clearly all wrong: some dreadful mistake. What he wanted above everything was to stay with me; and he knew by now that that was what I really wanted, too. So every time I firmly said "Stay!" and began to walk slowly away from him, he would look at me quizzically, as though I must have had some kind of brainstorm. After a few doubtful moments, he would invariably decide to trust his instincts, and come trotting expectantly after me as though he hoped that this was what I really wanted after all. Even if I was having an aberration, he was not going to desert me.

The solution to this dilemma was surprisingly easy: an appeal to his sense of responsibility. I discovered that if I combined the command "Stay!" with "On guard!", Bobbin would have far less difficulty in remaining at his post. Once he realised that he was expected to protect and watch over some article such as a glove or a handbag while I was unable to look after it myself, he was eager to show that he appreciated the importance of his role. Proud and alert, with his head held high, he would sit up beside the treasured possession until I returned to relieve him of his duty.

In spite of his early reluctance, I have always in later years been able to depend on him to stay where he is left whenever it really matters - as well as knowing that anything I leave beside him will be perfectly safe.

Bobbin was a diligent pupil, and always keen to please. Because much of our time was to be spent out riding, it was particularly important that he should learn to come to the heel of the pony when he was out of reach of the lead, and safety demanded it. He grasped this very quickly, and if ever I saw trouble or traffic ahead, I had only to call "Heel!" and I knew that Bobbin would be there in a flash, trotting cheerfully along just behind us.

He was just as quick to learn that he must stop at the edge of any road before crossing, and to sit patiently until he hears the command "Over!"; after which, he gallops across as fast as possible and in a straight line. But before long I noticed that while he was waiting, and whenever he approached any road, he would also look both ways to see if any cars were coming. I hadn't set out to teach him the Green Cross Code, but he seemed to absorb the rules instinctively, and I could count on the fingers of half a hand the number of times he has ever tried to cross a road without stopping and looking first. If ever we meet a vehicle unexpectedly, he promptly steps in to the side of the lane to let it pass.

Not everything went quite so smoothly. To my surprise - ignorant as I was - the lesson which was most troublesome for Bobbin was learning to walk on the lead. Everything else had been so easy, I hadn't given any thought to how strange this would be for him, and I shall never forget the first time when, in my innocence, I clipped his brand new leather lead on to his collar and walked out of the front gate. I had expected my little friend to trot contentedly along at my side, eager to follow wherever I chose to take him.

How wrong I was. I found, instead, that I had something resembling a demented fish on the end of a fly-cast line - a wriggling, twisting scrap of animation that would rather do anything than walk beside me. Progress was impossible: I couldn't tell whether he would be trussed up like a chicken or strangled first, as he leapt and rolled and side-stepped and bounced on the end of this alien umbilical cord. I was nonplussed. But of course it was not long before Bobbin worked out what to do; by the second day, he had mastered the required technique as confidently as he mastered everything else. Since then, on those rare occasions when it has been necessary to put him on a lead, he has walked with his head and tail held high, with an extra spring in his step, as though this arrangement were a special kind of honour.

But the compliance of even such an exemplary dog as Bobbin has its limits. There are some instincts in a Jack Russell's nature which even his desire to oblige his best friend will not suppress. While he has always been both happy and proud to demonstrate his understanding and willingness in almost every other situation, once he has got some special prize between his teeth, he simply cannot see why he should let it go. Knowing how sharp are those teeth, it seemed particularly important to instil obedience to the command "Leave!" for fear that one day he might close his vice-like jaws on a friend's best Dior scarf, or a small child's favourite teddy.

I still think we might have succeeded: Bobbin had been so biddable in every other way. But circumstances were against us. Everyone knows that the grip of a Jack Russell's teeth is so tenacious, and his jaw so strong, that if he has hold of a stick he will not let go even if you lift his feet clear of the ground and twirl him round by it. Too many friends found that they were unable to resist playing such a vigorous game of tug-of-war. It was just too tempting, and my cries of "Leave!" fell on ears that were too excited to listen.

For Love of a Dog

A dog's intelligence is such that whatever you may decide to teach him, it is certain that he will learn much, much more than ever you intended or expected - and almost certainly more than you will ever realise. I had set out to teach Bobbin a few simple words: "sit", "stay", "leave", "heel", "no" and "down". Like any other dog, he quickly learnt the meaning of other interesting words such as "dinner", "biscuit", "chew", and "walk". He also learnt phrases such as "Get up on the path", "Go in the garden", "bed time", "upstairs", "We're going out", "later", "wait" and many others. The list of words that I now know he can recognise, and understand, would take up pages; they include people's names, different types of food such as cheese and chocolate, words such as "dangerous" and "good boy" and "vet".

It is just as well that a dog is so intelligent. He lives with us in a peculiar and ambivalent relationship. At one moment we are ordering him to

"Sit!" or "Leave!", and apparently determined to brook no disobedience; the next, we are waiting on him hand and foot, kindly offering him ready-made meals on a tray and providing him with comfortable beds, tit-bits and toys. It is a complex relationship, and would probably be baffling to a dog, if he did not have so much talent for interpreting the caprices of our behaviour towards him. In fact, it seems that sometimes the dog may have a keener insight into this peculiar and ambiguous state of affairs than do we.

I like to believe that our relationship with our canine friend can incorporate a certain amount of give and take: total domination of a dumb animal seems an unappealing sort of goal. But there is one point on which absolute clarity must be established. Given that a dog is at heart a pack animal, it is always crucial to the success of our arrangement with him that there is no doubt about who is leader of the pack.

Some dogs seem to accept quite easily that the Human or Humans in the household are always the leaders; others need more assertive indications. It is for this reason that we are recommended by dog behaviourists to refrain from feeding Fido until we have finished our own meal. It is better, we are advised, to insist that Fido always stays on the floor, at a lower level than the rest of us. For many dogs this is enough; but as a last resort, it may be necessary for us to brush up on our command of dog language to press the point home beyond all reasonable doubt.

Like every terrier I have met, Bobbin has a decidedly independent character. Cooperative and obliging as he has always been, there was a brief moment in the early days when a slight question mark may have hovered over the matter of leadership. It seems only fair to tolerate the occasional drowsy grumble which says, "Leave me alone, I'm trying to sleep." We all feel like that sometimes. But any more demonstrative expression, such as bared teeth, is not to be encouraged.

There had been a few occasions when his disinclination to be woken in the mornings was becoming rather too apparent. I began to think I had perhaps been too tolerant of his irritation: I didn't like the sight of those teeth. Recollecting some advice I had once read in a dog-training manual, I decided to respond to Bobbin in his own language, just to make things clear. Getting down on my hands and knees (fortunately no one was watching) as fiercely as I could I bared my teeth and growled back at him. I even ventured so far as, very gently, to nip his ear.

The effect on Bobbin was electric. At once he became all licks and smiles, and he left me in no doubt about how sorry he was. That once was enough: Bobbin had learnt the lesson, and has never since forgotten who is leader of the pack in our house, when the chips are down. But if there is ever a moment of hesitation, then all I have to do is to bare my teeth....

There is no doubt that failure to be clear on this point can lead to all kinds of trouble. At least two husbands I know, both coincidentally with German Shepherd dogs in the house, find it almost impossible, or at least very risky, to share the matrimonial bed with their wives. Buster has taken a liking to the floral duvet, and to the kind ministrations of Mrs. Dog-Lover, and spares neither snarl nor growl in his campaign to reserve this favoured position for his exclusive enjoyment .... perhaps not a very good scenario. But then again, dogs are incredibly adept at picking up on their owners' subconscious feelings with ingenuous and guilt-free perceptiveness and accuracy.

Training a dog is a special time of closeness and enjoyment: the beginning of a life-time of working together. True training is far more than simply drilling a dog to obey instantly and without question any pre-arranged word of command you might choose to give. It is far more than simply ensuring that he never oversteps the boundaries of whatever it is that you think a dog should be and do. A clear system of communication is only one part of it. As with any other relationship, the most important element is the process of building up a mutual trust and understanding, which will underpin everything that you and your dog do together. If you succeed - and most dogs will do more than their fair share to help you - then the rewards are great. The unshakeable qualities of loyalty and devotion with which a dog will repay you are likely to make his friendship at least as delightful as any other you will know.

It is worth working at.

For Love of a Dog

Chapter 6: Building A Relationship

Looking back, it is almost impossible now to unpick those years of shared experience, or to define how it is that the closeness of unspoken mutual understanding has come about. Thousands of people watch *One Man and His Dog* and think how remarkable is the bond between man and animal. In his shepherding role, the dog is responding to the giving of specific learnt instructions, and his responses are built on instinctive pack behaviour. Yet a dog learns and understands so much more than this without any training or instruction at all, as every person who has been lucky enough to have the friendship of a dog will know.

In the fourteen years since that tiny puppy left his mother and settled in my house, we have both worked on building up a relationship. Each of us has learnt to recognise and respond to the other's moods and language, and gradually there has grown a depth of understanding which it is hard to define or explain. In retrospect, however, I can see that there were some particular circumstances, early on, which inevitably led to a greater closeness, and a strengthening of that bond on which so many years of friendship have been built.

The first was when Bobbin was still a tiny puppy called Fudge. When he was only ten weeks old, he was taken for his first visit to the vet, for round one of his immunisations - a perfectly routine procedure. What, if anything, went wrong I have never known, but within a few hours he was desperately ill. For thirty-six hours he did not stop vomiting, or trying to vomit, and he lay like a lifeless toy, limp and shivering, in my hands. I took him to the vet on Saturday and again on Sunday morning. He was unable to keep down any solid food, or even any water.

"Keep giving him water with the dropper. He must have some fluid or he'll have to go on a drip. Ring me at six o'clock this evening, and if he isn't better by then, we'll have to admit him."

My heart thudded miserably: the thought of such a defenceless little bundle of fur lying alone in a vet's hospital cage, attached to a drip, filled me with horror, and all day I nursed him carefully, keeping him warm and trying unsuccessfully to encourage him to swallow a drop or two of liquid without retching and being sick.

Fortunately, just before six in the evening, for the first time he swallowed down a teaspoonful of water without immediately bringing it up again. At last I began to dare to hope: perhaps he was, after all, going to recover. He had turned the corner. But those long hours of black and helpless anxiety had brought about some long-lasting changes. For a start, there was no more sleeping downstairs; for those two nights I had no choice but to have Bobbin not only upstairs, but in my bed. It was January, it was cold, and it was the only way to give his starved and shivering body some warmth. He was so weak that I had to help him stagger to his feet each time he wobbled around trying to be sick. From then on, I began to realise how fragile could be the thread of vitality which inhabited his vulnerable body: the closeness which arises from nursing a sick creature was here to stay.

This illness in fact had far-reaching effects for Bobbin; for several months he was able to digest only lean minced chicken, and all through his life he would thenceforth be visited by periodic bouts of digestive disorder which have needed careful monitoring and treatment. If I had ever been in danger of taking his health for granted, those days were quickly over.

The second vital factor in our relationship was that, once his immunisations were complete, and he had built up some muscle strength, Bobbin would be coming out daily with me when I rode my Welsh Cob, Cookie. It was vital that I could depend on him to respond quickly to any commands, since there would be times when it would be necessary to give first attention to the horse. It was also essential that from the very beginning he should always stay within sight: I had a dread of his disappearing down an unknown rabbit hole miles from home, somewhere along the downs.

I need not have worried. From his earliest visits to the field, and his first tentative rides in my pocket, he took to this way of life with enthusiasm and enjoyed every minute of his riding days. Cookie and I were his pack, or his family, and it was evidently just as important to him that he always stay close to us as it was to me not to lose sight of him. Wherever we happened to ride, Bobbin would always pursue his own canine adventures. He was a dog, and he lived his life as a dog, with his own special interests wherever we went: but he never forgot that he belonged to our team, and he had no intention of being left behind.

Fortunately, unlike so many of my friends' Jack Russells, he has never seemed in serious danger of disappearing down an inviting-looking rabbit hole. Maybe I was just lucky - he had, after all, come from 'working' parents - or perhaps, he, like me, had an instinctive mistrust of pot-holing. But from the first time he stopped to look longingly down the burrow of a recently escaped rabbit, I would shout at him in tones deliberately resonant with fear, "Don't go down there! Come away! It's DANGEROUS!" He would study my expression of alarm, and I could almost see his brain thinking, "Oh well, she may be right. It's probably not worth it. There are plenty more where that one came from." Perhaps he was glad of the excuse for not having after all to go down that ominously dark burrow. At any rate, he would back away and turn round with apparently cheerful indifference, and soon be off in search of a new adventure.

On his earliest walks, when he first was allowed off the lead, as soon as he had gone about twenty yards away from me, I would call him. He quickly understood what this meant, and knew that he did not need actually to come back to me, unless I insisted on it. All that was required was that he turn round and look at me to see what it was I wanted. After a quick glance to make sure that all was well, he would continue with his explorations. But he was never allowed to go out of eye or ear contact.

This system of keeping in touch became developed into such a fine art that sometimes he must have thought I was extremely slow-witted. If ever he temporarily disappeared from view, and I began to feel concerned, I would call him or whistle. Hearing the summons, Bobbin would at once pop his head obligingly out of the undergrowth, and stand patiently staring at me until I had spotted him. But if we were walking in the woods on a bright sunny day, a day of intense light and dark shadows, it might take me several minutes to realise that somewhere under a blackberry bush, round a bend in the path, a black and white muzzle which blended perfectly with the light and shade was patiently pointing in my direction.

"Oh there you are!" I'd cry when I finally discerned his twinkly eyes peeping at me from the midst of the shadows.

For Love of a Dog

Then with an ecstatic leap, Bobbin would bound out of the bushes and come racing up to me with a distinctly cheeky smile on his face, and rush off again with renewed exhilaration. He seemed to enjoy this joke of being able to keep a watchful eye on me while I couldn't see him - his own personal version of hide-and-seek, which he has continued to play time and time again, even in his more sedate old age.

Only once did I actually nearly lose him, and this experience, too, brought us closer together. While I was grooming and tacking up the pony, Bobbin would enjoy having some time to himself; he would mooch around the corners of the field, sniffing after foxes and seeing off the occasional rabbit. Occasionally I would hear him barking furiously as he flew down the steep bank through the woods in wild pursuit of his quarry. I would listen to know which way he had gone, but I didn't worry; the minute we were ready to go, he would be back at my side, eager to set off with us.

One evening he didn't come back when I called. We waited for ten minutes or so. But the daylight hours were short, and it would soon be too dark to ride. I began to tire of waiting, and confident that he would catch us up, as he always did, when he heard Cookie's hooves on the lane, we set off up to the downs.

But he didn't catch us up. I went on, feeling rather vexed, for a few more minutes; but still there was no sound of tiny claws on the tarmac racing up behind us. Everywhere began to seem horribly silent: no sound of dog or rabbit or activity anywhere. Suddenly feeling rather sick, I turned back and untacked the pony in the field. For the first time in two years, there was no response to my calling, and I tried hard to fight off the tides of panic. What could have happened? Had he at last decided to follow a rabbit into its burrow? He could be trapped anywhere in the tangled trackless undergrowth of Foxbury Shaw. There were only about one and a half hours of daylight left - how could I find him? Who would help? What if he was stuck? Or suffocating under a pile of collapsed earth somewhere underground? What if he had followed a deer further up the hill? Behind us the woods of the North Downs stretched for miles and miles. He could be exhausted, or lost, or injured. It was half a mile to the nearest road, but perhaps ... Or supposing he had found some poison? Would I be able to find him in time? Where should I start to look?

I called and called, almost unable now to keep the tears from my voice, and began as best I could to search the nearest parts of the woods. But the banks were so steep, and the ground so overgrown, that it would have been almost impossible to find even a larger animal.

For nearly two hours I continued searching and calling. With every minute that passed, I felt more lost and desolate. It was getting too dark to see properly, and I had almost come to the conclusion that I would not be able to find him that evening without a miracle, when I decided to look where I had not thought of looking before - in the narrow strip of woods immediately behind the stable. There were no rabbit holes here - the gap was only about two feet wide - and it was only a few feet from where I had been tacking up. Obviously, if he were here he would have heard me calling.

But there he was, his white outline glowing faintly in the half-darkness. He was standing up, quite still, apparently quite calm, just waiting. My instant relief was mixed at first with astonishment, and then the beginnings of anger. He was just standing there! Looking so calm! I was nearly demented and had been calling him for two hours! "You naughty dog .... !" The words trailed away into the twilight as at last I saw what had happened. There, passing through his collar, and wedged in the bank at either end, was a hazel pole. How it had managed to get there was difficult to imagine: but there it was. He could not have moved without choking himself.

I nearly sobbed as I struggled to release him. It was not only the immense relief of knowing that after all he would be coming home with me once again that night, but something more. In my desperation and exhaustion, for a few moments I had almost given up on him, and had certainly (I felt very ashamed) begun to doubt him. Had he ever, after all, failed to come when I had called him before? Yet it was quite clear from his expression of calm confidence that he had never for one moment doubted me, or given up hope. He had been absolutely certain that I would come. He must have thought I had been awfully slow about finding him. But his unshaken faith had kept him from struggling and possibly hurting himself further. Once again I was brought up short: another lesson to be learned and remembered, and to be illustrated many more times over the years: when it comes to faith and courage, we humans simply aren't in the same league as a Jack Russell.

Chapter 7: A Little Faith In My Friends

Few would dispute that of all the natural attributes of a dog, faith and trust are among the most enduring. It has been a source of growing wonder to me time and again to discover just how potent a force this unfailing instinct to trust can be. So often, we tend to think of faith as being somehow virtuous. Echoes of the high-flown spiritual exhortations from St. Paul's epistles float around in our heads: *'Faith, hope, and love, these three .... But the greatest of these is love...'*, and so on. It has to be acknowledged, however, that in all probability, the strength of a dog's faith may have more to do with expediency and survival; and is that, after all, so very different from humans? But whatever its motive, a dog's faith has, in my experience, at least as much hope as anyone else's of moving a mountain. In the matter of faith and trust, a dog is dogged.

In Bobbin's case, his total and unshakeable faith in humans manifests itself most visibly in respect of his dietary requirements. No one could ever describe Bobbin as a greedy dog; on the contrary, it has all too often been difficult to get him to eat at all. Many's the time I have had to tempt his appetite by hand feeding little morsels of freshly cooked chicken, until his digestive juices get going and he starts to eat up his breakfast.

There are people who believe it is all wrong to 'pander' to a dog in this way. "He's a dog," they say brightly. "If he's hungry, he'll eat." Perhaps; but a dog that is off-colour needs as much care as anyone else; and experience has shown time and again that if he doesn't get some food inside him he will not only go on feeling unwell, but will also be lethargic and shivery until he has had some nourishment. His metabolism in this respect works very like a young child's. When little Jamie is tired and crotchety, give him some food and soon you have a lively smiling infant once more, filled with a zest for life and mischief.

Nevertheless, it is true that not everyone takes this attitude. I have one friend, for example, whose vet had told her that a particular brand of dog food was really the only kind of food that should be given to dogs, and so she decided that that was what her dogs would eat. It worked quite well with her collie, who would (and did) eat anything, but the Yorkshire Terrier turned up her nose at it. Day after day she refused to eat.

"How worrying!" I said, thinking of how anxious I felt when Bobbin was off his food.. "What did you do?"
"I just gave her the same food every day until she ate it. I wasn't going to give in."
"How long did it take?"
"Oh, about a fortnight .... but I haven't had any trouble since then."

That is to say, no more trouble in getting her dogs to eat their Tinno; but then my friend does still have to keep the collie either muzzled or on a lead the whole time as otherwise she eats anything she can find, including many unmentionable deposits of other dogs and foxes. I can't help feeling that she might just be, perhaps understandably, trying to vary her diet.

Bobbin, on the other hand, is inclined to be rather too selective when it comes to eating. While he is very partial to chocolate (not that he often has the chance of this delicacy) he definitely does not like mint chocolates. On more than one occasion, a kind waitress in a pub, eager to offer our canine companion some tangible token of her esteem, has retired to the kitchen to fetch him an After Eight Mint. Bobbin sniffs the offering courteously, and then, literally, just turns up his nose at it. Apparently unaware of the hurtfulness of this rejection, he continues to look with unabashed hopefulness at his new admirer, in the sure belief that his preference for a chocolate *without* mint will eventually be understood.

This is where the faith comes in. He evidently does not for a moment doubt that his trust will be rewarded; and it is remarkable to what lengths some of his admirers will go in order to avoid disappointing him.

If he is present at a tea party, for example, although he is at a disadvantage in being out of sight down by our feet, his sense of smell will always inform him with uncompromising accuracy what is available. And he holds out for exactly what he likes best. Where biscuits are concerned, his order of preference goes something like this:

1 Chocolate digestive (definitely NO to Jaffa Cakes)
2 Treacle Crunch
3 Digestive
4 Malted Milk
5 Rich Tea.

If you offer him a rich tea biscuit and he can smell digestive biscuits, he simply refuses it politely and keeps on looking until you offer him the one he wants. Similarly, if his nose tells him that chocolate biscuits are on the table, a plain digestive simply isn't good enough.

Some people seem to be shocked at his choosiness - although they may be just as choosy themselves. But what else can he do? What would you do? You or I would be offered the plate, and could choose for ourselves; he has to wait to be asked time and again. But never for an instant does he lose faith that his wishes will eventually be recognised; and he waits meanwhile with a patience and politeness that would do credit to many people I have met. He simply sits and stares with a gaze so meek and trusting that it is almost impossible to ignore.

Bobbin's unwavering belief in the good intentions of his human associates is so persuasive that nine or more times out of ten, his faith is rewarded. He would have to be hard of heart indeed who could refuse the mute and gentle plea in those dark, appealing eyes. What a lesson to us all! A dog that leapt up at the table for food would be sent away in disgrace and get nothing. But there is no need for this: Bobbin knows his needs will be met by his friends; he has no doubts, and nor does he need to have. His simple faith achieves all.

If Bobbin is hungry, he doesn't make a fuss or bark; he just goes and lies quietly across the door of the refrigerator. And if he is getting depressed by the long wait, he curls up in a very small miserable-looking ball: his humility and resolute patience are irresistible.

It is not just a question of giving in to his whims; but this intense and unshakeable faith is something which I respect and treasure. As long as there is no good reason to refuse him, I would hate to betray that trust just as any parent would hate to see a six-year-old child go downstairs on Christmas morning and find nothing under the tree.

Although he is inclined to be naturally aloof with human beings to whom he has not been properly introduced, Bobbin has a very deep faith in his many friends. He is seldom disappointed, not only because his friends are worthy of his trust, but also because he has a remarkable memory of what each friend is likely to give him. Over the years, he has created his own pattern of social behaviour, and formed particular relationships with individual friends of mine - or as I should more correctly say, ours. When we go to visit Cynthia or Sue, he gets a Schmacko. At Betty and John's house he is always given a digestive biscuit: but before he leaves, he sits by the larder door until we remember the Kat Bits. At Dorothy and Denny's, he waits eagerly to be offered a cup of tea. Unfortunately, at Jeanne and Peter's he was once given a piece of ham - his very favourite food: now nothing else will do.

Bobbin's memory is long. One summer in Devon, we visited some friends whom we had not seen for years. Bobbin at once leapt out of the car in joyful recognition. After a quick look round the garden to check the scents, he was in the kitchen, sitting politely and staring intently up at the work surface. Very kindly, Jackie got out the biscuit tin; but no, he did not want a coconut crunch. Nor a drink of water. And while we drank our coffee, he refused to join us, maintaining his vigil alone on the cold kitchen floor.

Just as we were leaving, we remembered that when we had been here before, he had been offered some of the cat's Brekkies. Obligingly she took down the box and offered him a handful; and the perk of the ears and lift of his tail unmistakably said, "Thank you very much. That was just what I was hoping for!"

In any house we visit, even if he knows that there is nothing else on offer, he will go and sit quietly by the kitchen sink, whether or not he is thirsty. He knows that no one can refuse him a drink of water. Once this has been provided, he settles down, satisfied that he, too, has been given the ritual offering of hospitality.

But some places are very special: and Bobbin's excitement knows no bounds when we arrive at Pauline's, or Mary and Peter's; for here he is unfailingly given a dish of fresh goat's milk, which in his eyes is absolute heaven. Seeing his delight, I have several times bought a carton of goat's milk from Waitrose, or offered him a cup of tea, but it is not the same. And at home, he refuses to touch Brekkies. The savour for Bobbin of all these special treats derives not from their taste, but from the fact that they are a token of friendship - something given just to him.

Sometimes his understanding and memory take even me by surprise. One fine spring day, we were visiting my friend Moira when we decided to go for a walk. Bobbin was enjoying sunbathing on her Indian rug and made it clear by his demeanour that he was not keen on the idea of surrendering his sun spot for the rigours of exercise.

"Come on, Bobbin," said Moira persuasively, "Be a good boy and come for a walk, and when we get back I'll give you a piece of cheese."
Bobbin's ears pricked up at once - he has a particular liking for cheese - and he looked meaningfully at the fridge.
"When we come back," repeated Moira, "We're going for a walk first."

An hour or so later we returned from a pleasant ramble through bluebell woods, ready for a cup of tea. I am sorry to say, that what with this and that, we had both forgotten Moira's promise to Bobbin. But as soon as the front door was opened, he shot in and took up his position by the fridge with an air of eager expectancy. We went on chatting and getting the tea, and eventually Moira offered him a biscuit. He refused it, and began to look distinctly indignant. She offered him a saucer of tea, and I offered him a chew. He began to quiver and fidget his feet in that particular way he has when he is trying very hard not to get impatient with our stupidity. Suddenly we remembered - cheese!
"I said I'd give him a piece of cheese!" said Moira.

At the sound of the magic word, he sprang to his feet and stood back so that Moira could open the door of the refrigerator.
"Do you think he could actually have remembered?" asked Moira in amazement.
We couldn't think of any other explanation.

Whether or not the extraordinary intensity of faith shown by a dog towards his two-legged friends is laudable in moral terms is perhaps irrelevant. What is beyond dispute is the powerful effect that the constancy of this faith - a faith which does not leave room for a shadow of a doubt - has on those who come into contact with it. Disappointment becomes unthinkable. The potency of those steadily gazing eyes, and the process of thought transference are irresistible.

And why should they be resisted? They bring out the best in those around. The mute, unwavering trust brings out in most people a desire to understand the dog's language, and to think of his requirements for a moment, as well as their own. For Bobbin, it is an extremely effective means of communication - as well, of course, as being the only way of expressing what he needs: but it is necessarily a two-way process.

There will always be some people who respond by getting on their high horse about how dogs should be kept in their place - people who apparently believe that while in their presence, a dog should as far as possible try not to be at all noticeable, and should certainly not be allowed in any way to attract any of the attention which they feel should more properly be directed to themselves. But this attitude somehow seems to provide a more enduring insight into their personality than into Bobbin's; and I have to say that the humans do not show up too well in the comparison.

Fortunately, there are a great many more people who are glad to respond to the humble, trusting neediness of a dumb animal. To a dog, we can show affection, talk kindly and gently, and offer gifts without fear of rejection (unless it happens to be Bobbin and an After Eight Mint). It can be so much less threatening and so much more satisfactory to make friends with a dog. Most people are glad to be generous; and the act of giving and receiving brings contentment and satisfaction to both parties. The trust of the dog arouses kindliness in his human friend, and the benefit is mutual.

We have very few friends left who cannot have patience with the simple requests of a dumb animal; one way or another our ways have parted. Whether human or canine, I prefer the company of the generous and warm-hearted - and who would not?

For Love of a Dog

Chapter 8: Meeting Other Dogs

Like many dogs, Bobbin has always had a knack of making friends wherever he goes; and he has met few people who have not been won over by his huge eyes and steady, intelligent gaze. He is not a dog to be ignored. My neighbour, who is renowned throughout the town as a misanthropic eccentric, with a particular aversion to dogs, threatened all kinds of hideous and illegal fates for Bobbin when we first moved in next door to him. But after a couple of years, even he volunteered one day that he "liked my little dog." To reinforce his point, he added that Bobbin was the "smartest thing" about me, and he couldn't understand how someone like me came to have such a nice little dog - I was flattered! This extraordinary accolade seemed proof indeed that Bobbin has what might be described as charisma, even if I have not.

This is nothing unusual in dogs. There has been increasing recognition in recent years of the evidence that dogs have a therapeutic effect on human beings. Schemes set up to introduce dogs to hospital visiting have achieved remarkable results. Just one example was the case of the autistic little girl who was unable to relate to anyone until she began to form a relationship with a visiting golden retriever; and it is widely recognised that people who have pets recover more quickly from major operations, and are less likely to fall victim to certain types of illness. Few who are familiar with dogs could fail to notice the health-giving effect that they have on those in contact with them, in so many different ways and so many situations.

But Bobbin's ability to win friends wherever he goes is not restricted to humans. It is equally noticeable in his encounters with fellow dogs and other members of the animal kingdom. Even dogs who are alleged by their owners not to get on with other dogs seem to find him acceptable or even endearing, and unfriendly encounters have been rare.

For me it has been a privilege and a source of endless fascination to observe his approaches and exchanges with other animals: a study from which I have learnt much about social interaction in dogs - much that often seems to be transferable to human behaviour. Humans and dogs have many things in common. Both are, in the main, pack animals, and therefore both have the same fundamental needs in terms of social intercourse: being accepted, making friends, and equally important, identifying and dealing with enemies. The most marked difference, as far as I can see, is the directness and candour with which dogs conduct the process of getting to know each other, and the corresponding honesty of their behaviour.

Anyone who has ever watched a dog closely cannot fail to be impressed by the manner in which our canine friends prepare to meet or greet each other. Bobbin's techniques have varied and developed over the years, but the central core of method and purpose are unchanging. The primary aim is to find out what the other dog is like, and in particular, whether this stranger is going to be an ally or a foe. (Isn't this also what human beings are always trying to learn about each other?) To this end, therefore, when an approaching stranger is spotted, the first thing a dog will do is to stand quite still and fully alert. Using all his senses and knowledge about body language, he learns as much as possible before he draws any closer.

Younger dogs may take a while to learn this piece of canine social etiquette, and often an adolescent dog will bounce enthusiastically up to the new dog in a boisterous way, perhaps circling round him as if wanting a game. Such ill-mannered advances may be repelled with an abrupt rebuke by an older dog, who prefers to preserve the decorum of social convention. Sometimes, if both the dogs are older, or slightly nervous, or when perhaps the signals given and received are not sufficiently clear, neither will be willing to make the first move. Only rarely does this sizing up from a distance develop into such a long drawn out 'stand-off' that, as a last resort, the humans have to step in as leaders of the pack and go first to encourage their companions to be brave.

The basic rule of the stand-off is that each dog continues to face the other until they feel ready for closer contact. Without any need for words, the message is quite clear: "I can see you. I am standing my ground. I am just making up my mind .... What are your signals?" The most decisive scenario occurs if one or other dog turns its back during a stand-off. This 'backing down' is universally recognised as a sign of fear and desire to escape, and is a blatant acknowledgment of defeat.

One day, we were out walking on a popular piece of local common land when a boxer dog suddenly shot out of the bushes in front of us. Both Bobbin and the boxer were taken aback at this precipitate encounter, and promptly froze. The stand-off was still unbroken when the boxer's owner evidently began to wonder where he was, and called him from a path further up the hill. Boxer heard the summons and responded at once by racing off to find his owner.

To Bobbin, this sudden departure was a sign of an unexpectedly easy victory: Boxer had been unable to withstand his gaze and had run away! Normally so cautious in his mature years, now Bobbin was exultant: he had won! And without hesitation he charged off after the boxer, confident now that here was no threat. He had no plans to be aggressive; he simply had wanted to be sure that he would not be out-manoeuvred before advancing further. Boxer now realised that his retreat had been rather hasty, so he had to turn back and meet his pursuer. Without more ado, the two dogs proceeded to exchange ritual greetings: having selected a suitable tree trunk, they took turns to scent-mark it, three times each. Honour was satisfied; and both were then able to continue in their separate directions.

If the stand-off is allowed to run its course, then in due time one or other will begin to indicate by his body language, tentatively at first, that he is ready to move a little closer. He may begin ever so slightly to quiver his tail (active wagging is reserved for a meeting with someone specially attractive, and is far more committing) and indicate a willingness to move a few inches towards the other. Usually the other will at this point reciprocate, and the speed at which they approach each other is determined by a number of factors such as their age, temperament and sex.

That is, if they are going to make friends. If one of the dogs begins to raise its hackles or growl, then the outlook may be different: these can be signs that an enemy is in sight, and it may be best for the leader of the pack to intervene and keep a safe distance between them. But trouble is rare: dogs are instinctively so skilled at establishing the ground rules for a relationship, especially when they are off the lead and free to manoeuvre.

It is important for dogs to find out what they can about a stranger before meeting, and to have time and space to do so. And in this respect, we humans are not so very different. When we are going to meet someone new, don't we too try to find out something about them, if possible before we meet, or certainly as soon as possible thereafter? We are always longing to ask such basic questions as "Where do you live? What do you do? Are you in a relationship?" because the answers are our indicators of the potential compatibility, or usefulness, of the new contact. If we are socially adept, we will fight shy of asking such directly intrusive questions, and try instead to discover the answers through subtler means: we don't want to look as if we might have anything to lose or gain by the comparison or the exchange. But, whatever our means, our goal of getting information rarely differs.

It is to me a constant source of wonder to reflect on how a dog can find out all he needs to know from a distance of perhaps fifty yards. I am sure that their finely tuned sense of smell plays its part; certainly difference in size, in itself, is not an automatic barrier. In fact, a small dog may perceive a larger dog as a useful potential ally. Bobbin, to my amazement, has never been deterred from embarking on friendship with a Great Dane or an Irish Wolfhound which may be seven or eight times his size. A pack needs all sorts of skills to be successful; allies who have different strengths may be all the more desirable.

A great deal of information is transmitted through a dog's complex body language - the stance of the legs, angle at which the head is held, and particularly the posture of the tail. A tail held high denotes confidence and excitement, and a willingness to exchange greetings. The more confident or eager a dog is, the higher and straighter he will hold both his head and his tail, thus indicating confidence, and offering as unrestrictedly as possible his personal scent.

Conversely, a drooping tail may denote fear, uncertainty, or desire to be left alone. If you watch closely, you can see each dog making minute adjustments to the positioning of his tail, his ears, and his back in invitation or response to similar adjustments of the other.

Now that Bobbin is older, and therefore more cautious, he almost invariably adopts the stand-off method of encounter. But when he was younger, he had a far more varied repertoire of approach. It was almost impossible to anticipate which method he would adopt in any given circumstances, or to analyse why. Sometimes, he would lie down flat in the grass and wait, ears alert, for the other dog to get closer, watching his every movement with sharpened eyes. Then, at the last minute, he would spring up with an expression of unmistakable enthusiasm, as if this ambush were a kind of game. At other times, after a quick glance, but without any apparent signs of fear, he would execute a wide detour to avoid going near the other dog. And every now and again, he would take almost no notice at all of an unfamiliar dog, walking by with his nose busily to the ground as though he knew this one was just not worth bothering with.

Once the distance learning is done with, it is common knowledge how dogs proceed to find out the things that really matter about each other. Some owners seem to find it embarrassing to let darling Alice have her bottom sniffed, or to see Rufus investigating the private parts of an unknown lurcher. After all, we humans do our sniffing in a far more refined and coded fashion - in public, at least. But this behaviour is so essential and intrinsic an element of being a dog and identifying with other dogs that it seems almost to amount to cruelty to attempt to interfere with such natural interactions. For all the rest of the day a dog must live as a kind of surrogate human, which is unnatural enough; surely he may be allowed to be a dog for just one part of the day? Surely, once in a while, the human owner may, as it were, try seeing things from the dog's point of view. Most do; those few who don't, are in my view missing out on a lot of the fun of having a partnership with a dog.

I have certainly learnt a great deal from Bobbin. The essence of his 'charisma', or ability to avoid conflicts and somehow hit the right note with each different dog he encounters seems to stem from his ability to convey through his body language just the right balance between submissiveness and threat - as well as a willingness to be patient. Once again, there may be a lesson here that we can learn from our canine companions. We humans are far more prone to have relationship problems than our dogs are. Perhaps we, too, should skip the soul searching, and just try to aim for the candid caution and simple honesty of the dog.

To watch the gentle, tentative way Bobbin approaches someone he is not quite sure of is a lesson in itself. With tiny movements of head and ears, with hesitant wags of the tail, and the occasional stamping of a paw, he uses every fibre of his being to encourage the other to respond. He never invades the other's personal space, he never tries to rush things. If Fido seems untrusting and a little aggressive, Bobbin stands still; he does not droop his tail in submission, but he offers no threat, and perhaps there may be a hint of a little wagging in his tail.

This non-threatening stance offers Fido the space he needs to think things out, until, in his own time, he is able to decide that he supposes he might as well just have one sniff of this little dog who is standing so still that you can almost *feel* the vibrations of friendliness emanating from his every muscle. Anyone who has watched two dogs, big or small, gently sniffing each others' nostrils, one paw uplifted, tail quivering, can scarcely doubt the tenderness of which a canine is capable.

There is no doubt that, like people, some dogs are more sociable than others. Bobbin has been lucky in that he has seldom had to suffer the restraints of a lead. For most of his life his walks have been in the company of the pony and myself, in safe open country, and he has been a free agent in his meetings with other dogs. Dogs who spend a lot of time on the lead seem to have a more limited language with which to conduct exchanges with others of their species, and perhaps have to miss out on meetings which, judging from Bobbin's obvious enjoyment, are often the highlight of his walk.

Perhaps charisma doesn't have anything to do with it; perhaps Bobbin through his travels has acquired a wide range of social graces. Perhaps dogs achieve different levels of social aplomb just as humans do.

But whatever his degree of charisma, or his social finesse, I cannot help respecting Bobbin's unpretentiousness: the straightforwardness with which he makes a quick and honest decision. It is either: "Nice to meet you but I don't think we were meant for each other," or else, "I really like you! Let's have a game and get to know each other better!" Either way there's none of the nonsense we humans indulge in, smiling with a crocodile smile and paying false compliments:
 "So lovely to see you, darling! We must do lunch!"

Give me the simple honesty of a dog any day.

Chapter 9: A Dog's Senses

For a young healthy dog, every inch of the world that he treads is a step towards adventure. Everywhere he goes, a dog finds excitement and information which is simply inaccessible to human beings. While we walk stolidly along the path, keeping our eyes fixed on the middle distance, stopping occasionally to look at a wild flower or perhaps greet a friend, often our thoughts are preoccupied with planning the shopping list, or the schedule for the week ahead. But our dog lives fully and firmly in the present moment, making the very most of every message and hint of interest that comes his way.

This ability to live in the here and now is an example for us all: something from which I, for one, have learnt a valuable lesson. How much of our precious time is spent going over again and again what is past and done with, or worrying about what might happen! Endlessly we try to work out what we should do, with our money, or lack of it, with our relationships, or with our lives. Our dog does none of this. He doesn't waste energy on fruitless regrets, or spend his prime time - the time of the present moment - on planning for the future. He looks around at where he is, and starts from there, each day of his life, and lives each moment, just as it is, now. Through the constant use of his highly-developed senses, he makes the most of all the stimuli around him, all the time.

And what senses he has! It is no secret that a dog's sense of smell is thousands of times more sensitive than a human's, and that his sense of hearing enables him to pick up sounds well before they come within the range discernible by our ears. How many times has Bobbin heard a friend's car turning in at the end of the road, and thus given me a few minutes' warning before the knock at the door! How many times, when we are walking alone in some remote corner of the countryside, has he pricked up his ears and stopped, suddenly alert, giving me timely warning that someone else is around, long before I should have heard or seen anything myself. And he can tell exactly where a mouse has crossed the path long after it has disappeared from view.

Since a dog's hearing is so sensitive, it could become a problem if he were to bark at every sound, and could not distinguish human friend from human foe. But like many other domestic dogs, Bobbin has always, from the very first, somehow known how to respond appropriately in different circumstances. And so, through combining our different skills and areas of knowledge, a useful partnership arose completely naturally: the primeval partnership between man and dog. Bobbin quickly learned to recognise not only the distinctive sound of my car's engine, but also those of our near neighbours and our friends. I, in my turn, eventually learned to recognise his different responses to these sounds; and so, together, with no word spoken, we found a way to be prepared for most situations.

When a car goes past our house, Bobbin's reaction varies according to what he knows about that particular car. If it is a neighbour's car, he acknowledges it by half pricking his ears, without moving his head; if it is a friend's car, he leaps up, rushes to the door and waits, head held high and ears alert for the imminent arrival. If it is one of his particular friends, he begins quivering with excitement. But if the car is one which he does not recognise, as soon as he hears its engine, his head and ears are raised, and he waits, motionless, and listening with full attention, for what will transpire. If the car stops outside our house, he at once starts to bark - one of the very few occasions when he does so, and a very sure indication to other pack members that they had better get ready for action. If the car stops a little way up the road, he continues on full alert until he is sure that the danger has passed. He is rarely concerned without cause, and although I have sometimes misinterpreted his signals, I don't think that his deciphering of the sound outside has ever erred.

The information that Bobbin gives me is extremely useful, and at times very reassuring. At night, for example, when it is possible for the wakeful to imagine that all kinds of strange sounds bring unwelcome threats (was that a branch tapping on the window? Or is it a sinister midnight visitation?) Bobbin can set my mind at rest, or otherwise, with his superior understanding. Not only can he distinguish whether a sound is made by a living thing, or simply by the wind or a door closing somewhere else, but he also knows what sort of living thing is out there in the dark. He appears to be able to pick up this information in any weather conditions, and regardless of whether windows and curtains are open or closed.

If he knows that outside there is a cat, then he goes nearly wild with barking, frantic to be let out so that he can chase this personal adversary off the face of the earth. If it is a fox, his growls are more low and menacing, and his expression takes on an altogether darker look: an alien enemy species is invading his territory. But if it is a human intruder, nothing will pacify him; he barks in a seriously threatening manner, and makes it clear by baring his teeth and by his aggressive stance that he understands that this intrusion threatens the whole pack.

The lane where we live is quietly situated, on the edge of a country town, and apart from cats and foxes we seldom get unwelcome intruders in the middle of the night. In fact, I would have said never, had it not been for two events in recent years which proved me wrong - and Bobbin right. On both occasions, in the middle of the night, when I was sound asleep, Bobbin suddenly woke up and started barking furiously, with that unmistakable note in his voice which said, "There's someone out there, in our garden! Someone who shouldn't be there! Let me out and I'll see to it!"

Perhaps because I was so tired that I didn't relish being woken in this way, or perhaps just because we humans are so stupid, I refused to listen to him. Instead I put my head under the pillow and kept telling him to be quiet. But Bobbin was adamant that there was danger in our garden, and he refused to be pacified. With steadfast resolution I ignored his repeated warnings, and at last I managed to get back to sleep. Much later, seeing that his best efforts were to no avail - and that the danger had passed - Bobbin also quietened down.

When we got up the next morning I found out that Bobbin had been right. On the first occasion, there on my front doorstep was a cigarette lighter which did not belong to me, and had not been there when we came home at midnight. On the second occasion, I discovered a distinctive, but unfamiliar, pen dropped in the garden. Of course I never knew who had been wandering around at two o'clock in the morning, let alone why. But since then I have been considerably more appreciative of how lucky I am to have a dog who is able to tell me when something is wrong. It is not his fault if I am too foolish to pay attention to his warnings.

This acute sense of hearing can of course be useful to a dog in a wide range of different circumstances. For example, Bobbin can hear a fridge door being opened no matter where he is in the house or garden - just as he can hear the opening of any tin, or the mention of the word 'ham'. This miraculous development of the sense of hearing has clearly evolved with the aim of maximising the chances of survival, and is an extension of the ability of a hunting dog to hear the smallest movement made by potential prey. But at times, we humans, with our inferior capacities, can find ourselves out-manoeuvred.

On one occasion we called to see a colleague, Judy, whose house we had not visited before. Judy started to make some coffee, and naturally went to the fridge to get out some milk. As usual, there was Bobbin, quick as a flash, peering anxiously in to check the contents. The fridge was almost empty, but not quite: there on the middle shelf was a large bar of chocolate. Bobbin licked his lips with anticipation and looked at Judy with meaningful affection.
"Sorry, Bobbin, you can't have that! It's Simon's."

While we sat in the living room and continued to chat over our coffee, Bobbin, who was clearly disappointed at being offered only a biscuit, lay down with an offended air, and pointedly turned his back on us.

Simon meanwhile had been out doing some shopping, and after about half an hour, I heard the front door open as he returned. To my surprise, Bobbin made no move to deter this intruder as he normally would have done: he was still feeling disappointed about the chocolate. But his silence was short-lived. A few moments later, Bobbin suddenly leapt up, and rushed madly into the kitchen, barking as if his life depended on it. I quickly followed. Sure enough, Simon had gone to the fridge and, yes, taken out the bar of chocolate. Bobbin had never met Simon before, and what he saw now made it clear that Simon was a burglar of the worst sort - the sort that goes straight for the chocolate. Having been denied this simple treat, Bobbin had not bothered to warn us when the intruder first entered the premises. But to allow him actually to steal the chocolate was more than any self-respecting Jack Russell could be expected to suffer in silence.

It is not easy for the average human to share in the delights of a dog's sense of smell. We simply do not have the equipment to appreciate the extent and complexity of the information that is transmitted to him through his marvellous nose. Each morning when we go out, each time we come home, Bobbin has to do a ritual tour of the stretch of lane outside our house, carefully sniffing each clump of grass for clues as to who has gone by since he last checked. Over some smells he lingers, vibrating his nostrils as though wishing to find out all that he possibly can about the visitor. When we go for a walk, every inch of the way must be examined for that vital information about what has been going on. This is a world I cannot enter; but just as I explore my world through newspapers, radio and the television, so I respect Bobbin's need to explore his. Where our worlds can overlap, it is exciting to share; but where they cannot, he can at least be allowed to enjoy his canine faculties to the full.

For Love of a Dog

We may not be able to discover much about a dog's world through our sense of smell, but certainly Bobbin, like any other dog, loses no chance of finding out unexpected things about ours. Everyone we meet is given a cursory sniff of the trousers as a quick check, and then usually dismissed as being rather boring - unless they live with a cat or dog, in which case the 'reading' of the trousers will be more detailed. But there are times when we have all had to marvel at the proof of Bobbin's olfactory powers.

One evening, at my parents' house, we were all relaxing quietly after dinner, when Bobbin suddenly got up and went across to my father's desk. Sitting down in front of it, he began that nose-pointing deliberate stare technique which means, "There is something very interesting in there. Please open it and I will show you ...."

"But there's nothing in there," my father said. "Only papers."

Bobbin went on staring; and rare are those who can resist that single-minded, concentrated stare. So after a few minutes my father went over and opened one of the drawers.
"You see?" he said, "Nothing at all." But Bobbin was not satisfied.

My father, who is secretly more fond of dogs than he likes to admit, began to empty out the drawers, putting the piles of paper on the floor. Bobbin carefully checked each of these, but continued to look expectant and determined. Finally, as the very last pile of papers was removed from the last drawer, right at the back, much to our mirth, was revealed a long-hidden Mars bar, no doubt squirrelled away at some time when my father was supposed to be on a diet. We all felt that Bobbin deserved at least a little piece of it.

For much of the time man and dog live side by side in separate worlds. When we go for our walks, Bobbin is no doubt puzzled by my interest in a particular orchid; and I probably disappoint him by being unaware of the fascination of an exotically scented piece of bracken. But there is one enjoyment which we can both share: when we reach the top of a hill, Bobbin is as delighted as I am to stop for a while and simply gaze at the view. Ever since he was a tiny puppy, he has loved to get to the summit of any eminence - be it hill, or mound, or even a tree stump - and with evident satisfaction survey the world from his newly acquired position of superiority. Obviously, if you are only fourteen or so inches off the ground, the opportunity to gain such additional height is not to be lightly passed up. From up here you can better look out for predators, scan the countryside for a glimpse of your prey .... or simply feel that you are king of all the world.

I know that there are very fundamental instincts in all animals which prompt them to seek a good vantage point; and these instincts are almost certainly more than ninety percent responsible for Bobbin's love of heights. I, on the other hand, like to think that I love to gaze at a view for aesthetic reasons - and to see more clearly a larger stretch of the landscape I am in. Why? I suspect that my sense of satisfaction, too, has its roots in a very primitive instinct for safety. Did not our most ancient ancestors choose the ridges of hills for their tracks and their camps?

For Love of a Dog

There have been many times when I have wished I could share with Bobbin in the secret pleasures he finds through his finely-tuned senses, or that I too could know what information it is that he finds so absorbing as he closely studies the fragrance of a stone. I must accept that I never shall share this rich and tempting world. There may be many things that Bobbin, too, wishes he could understand. And we have some consolation: by pooling our resources, we can build a partnership which works for the protection and satisfaction of both man and his best friend.

Yet when we have climbed a hill, and when we rest on the top, gazing wordlessly at the view, it seems to me that in that moment dog and man are perhaps most closely sharing the same enjoyment: a feeling of safety, of freedom, and of achievement that satisfies our deepest common instincts; and a feeling of being, for just that moment, on top of the world, together.

Chapter 10: Meetings By The Way

When first that little puppy, who didn't even yet have a name, left his mother's milky warmth, he stumbled out into a world that was full of exciting adventures, just waiting to be lived and explored by him. Anything and everything that he came upon was there to be investigated. Spurred on by his boundless curiosity and kept on the trail by his keen senses, he set out on a lifetime of discovery which has been as delightful to me as it is engrossing, and at times perplexing, to him.

Gradually, as he has met each new situation and tested it out, he has built up an understanding of how the world works; an understanding which is as unique to him as mine is to me. I do not know if he has formed any theories as to whether the earth is round or flat, but he has made discoveries and formed opinions (usually very valid) about the strange foibles of human behaviour, and the intricate subtleties of canine social behaviour. But some of his most endearing adventures have arisen from his early encounters with a variety of animals of different species.

In these encounters, too, Bobbin has often displayed not only an innocent curiosity and natural friendliness, but also what has appeared at times to be a kind of innate wisdom and gentleness, typical of his approach to the world. Above all, especially when he was still in that joyous period of extreme youthfulness, he investigated each new situation with a wonderful sense of spontaneity, optimism and fun. Jack Russells seem especially designed for fun - and to have an instinctive desire to seek opportunities for having a prank wherever they happen to find themselves.

Take the pheasant, for example. Bobbin can't have been more than six months old when one day we were visiting a friend. While Maggie and I were getting the horses in, Bobbin was having a delicious adventure, exploring all the scents of rabbit up and down the paddock. Suddenly he came to an abrupt stop, and crouched down low, barking as if he had discovered something worth looking at. At first I could not see what it was that was causing all this excitement; but as I drew closer I saw that squatting in the long grass, seeking in vain to hide, was a large fluffy baby pheasant. It sat there, blinking miserably, and looking completely bemused, while Bobbin raced round and round it, first clockwise, then anticlockwise, barking furiously.

Thinking that the pheasant must somehow be injured, I ran across the field, and shouted to Bobbin to leave it. Any minute, I thought, he would tire of these appetising overtures, and would pounce, and there would be an end of the unfortunate bird.

Every now and again, Bobbin would stop his circling, and put his head on one side quizzically. As I drew nearer, I saw that his tail was wagging hesitantly, and in between occasional puzzled glances at me, he would wrinkle up his nose at the pheasant, and yelp at it in what was, I now realised, a reproachful rather than an aggressive manner. Suddenly it dawned on me that he was not thinking of devouring this sorry creature: he was merely urging it to join him in his uproarious game. Much to his surprise, though not to mine, the poor bird had no idea at all of such a thing: and the more it continued to crouch forlornly into a huddled ball of ruffled feathers, the more frustrated Bobbin became. Why would not this playmate play?

Poor Bobbin! And poor pheasant! I had in the end forcibly to lead Bobbin away for fear that his zeal might overcome his restraint, or shock the benighted creature into an untimely demise. After about ten minutes of getting its breath back, the errant fledgling set off unsteadily back towards its cover; while Bobbin, disappointed in his hopes for a more stimulating game, returned to his pursuit of rabbit scent.

This approach, of believing that every living thing he met was a potential playmate, has seemed always to be the keynote of his encounters. Of course, there were some exceptions, and some hard lessons that had to be learned. When we were out riding, we would often be near farms and could never be sure what farm animals we might find around the corner. It was essential that Bobbin should learn early on not to chase those farmyard animals which are taboo - most particularly sheep, and chickens.

While Bobbin seemed always to want to make friends with everyone, rather than chase them, it is of course quite a different matter if an animal starts to run away. In his own interests as well as theirs, Bobbin must be trained never to a pursue even those notorious cowards who would instantly turn tail at his approach. 'DOGS CAUGHT WORRYING SHEEP WILL REGRETFULLY BE SHOT'. The warning, which Bobbin could not read, was posted at the entrance to many of the fields we habitually rode through.

It is not always practicable to put a dog on the lead when one is riding, and so I had to be able to place total trust in Bobbin never to be tempted to pursue these vulnerable creatures. I consulted my friend Pauline, a sheep farmer whose knowledge about all varieties of animals has been a source of assistance on more than one occasion.

"Bring him down here," she said, "My ewes have just lambed. We'll pop him in a pen with a couple of them and that should sort him out."
So the next week I took poor unsuspecting Bobbin down to Devon, where he was to learn his first really tough lesson.

When Bobbin saw the sheep, he thought they looked great fun. His ears pricked up and his eyes sparkled as if he anticipated having a really special game with so many interesting pals to play with. Little did he know that we had other plans.

Half way up the hill was a small stone sheep fold, and into this Pauline put a ewe with her twin lambs, who were just a week old - both of them already larger than Bobbin, though still quite a bit more wobbly. Then Bobbin was lowered in beside them, while we stayed outside ... and oh, I did feel sorry for him! This was much worse than the pheasant! Not only did both sheep and lambs refuse to play, but the ewe began by stamping her feet at him in an obviously aggressive fashion; and when Bobbin failed to retreat (which he was quite unable to do until we rescued him) she began to run at him with stabbing head butts. Bobbin simply stood there, looking baffled, and trying to duck the onslaughts; but each time the ewe backed off a little, he optimistically continued to wag his tail and make tentative sniffing advances which were quite clearly intended to be overtures of friendship. It was pitiful to behold.

I don't think we left him there for more than a few minutes; and I remember that Bobbin bore this disappointing reception with such stoical resilience and so little diminution of optimism that I doubted whether he would really have got the message. But Pauline seemed quite confident that enough was enough: and certainly Bobbin's subsequent impeccable comportment with sheep has proved her judgement right. In future, whereas he continued to show no fear of any other living creature, great or small (except bluebottles, and later flies), when he saw a field of sheep, his tail would at once go down, and he would hurry as fast as he could to escape from their proximity. This was exactly what was needed: it meant we could ride through a field of sheep, knowing that however much the sheep might run, Bobbin would go through like an arrow, glancing neither to right nor to left, and trying with all his courageous Jack Russell heart to conceal the fact that he feared that at any moment these ferocious beasts would turn and attack him.

I have always felt that we played a rather mean trick on Bobbin that day in the sheep fold. But the lesson was a very necessary one for his own protection. And so effective was this simple piece of schooling, that I even have a photograph, taken some years later, of Bobbin being chased by two young lambs. We were riding down a track towards the farm, and Bobbin was a little way ahead when suddenly a pair of black lambs wriggled out of their field straight into his path. For a moment I was anxious: should I dismount and pick him up, just to make sure that he wasn't tempted to forget the rules? Could he possibly resist such a blatant invitation right there in front of him to have a spot of fun?

Bobbin and the lambs stopped and stared at each other. I had my camera to hand, and even as I hesitated, one of the lambs took a step towards him. Too late! I thought. To my astonishment, instead of advancing to meet it, Bobbin turned tail and started to race back up the track towards us. No doubt he had recollected his earlier encounter with sheep, and was not going to risk trying to embark on any kind of a game again. From then on, it was very clear that Bobbin could always be trusted around sheep.

Dealing with the question of chickens was even easier - especially as Bobbin was such a quick learner. When he was about a year old, we went to stay with friends Pat and Malc. Their stable yard is in the heart of the Sussex weald, a lovely spot, set among quiet meadows, briar hedges and ancient oak trees; and all around the large yard and garden Pat's chickens run free range. The protected status of farmyard fowl was an issue which must be tackled without delay. As Bobbin set off friskily to explore the extent of the premises, I followed him, waiting to observe his reactions to seeing hens at such close quarters.

At first he was too busy concentrating on checking the smells, but once he knew the basics about his new territory, he began to let off steam by racing round and round the sand schools and paddocks, as if there were no greater joy in life than running. Suddenly, as he galloped round a corner, he came upon a hen and nearly knocked it down. It fluttered off, and Bobbin, looking rather startled, made to pursue it.

"No!" I shouted as fiercely as I could, "Leave it!" Bobbin gave the bird a regretful glance and then came racing back towards me. As we passed a few more chickens, I gave him a warning look and repeated this injunction in tones that were intended to imply all the horror of the consequences of doing otherwise.

Bobbin quickly realised that this was something that mattered. He gazed deep into my eyes with that serious, attentive expression which means that he is listening carefully and thinking as hard as a Jack Russell can. And from then on he made no more attempts to chase a chicken.

Later in the afternoon, we were sitting on the lawn. I was reading a book and Bobbin was keeping guard beside me, when some chickens began to wander towards us. As the first one approached, just for a moment Bobbin started to look alert as if he might be tempted. "No!" I said very firmly, "You are not allowed to chase chicken!" He looked at me with a hurt look as much as to say, "Yes, I know, you told me already. I only wanted to watch them." And after that he lay down on the grass, and all afternoon the hens scratched and pecked around us with impunity. It was quite clear that Bobbin had already learnt this lesson.

The trouble was, he had learnt *exactly* what I had taught him; and all went well until a little later that day a pair of ducks waddled towards us. Bobbin didn't hesitate for a moment. All afternoon he had restrained himself, and ignored every fowl that crossed his path, but he seemed to know straight away that these weren't chickens! In a flash, he leapt up and with a menacing bark lunged at the poor birds who had walked unsuspectingly almost into his jaws. I think I almost stunned him as I thumped the nearest part of him with my book, and yelled, "And not ducks either!"

Bobbin learned his lessons well. He soon knew that if a pheasant or rabbit starts up from under his nose, there is no reason why he should not have some fun chasing it. But farmyard fowl and sheep are in a different category: they must be accepted, ignored, and never pursued.

But the reason that Bobbin was so quick to learn these rules was because of his over-riding instinct to work cooperatively as a member of the pack. And rules or no rules, when he senses that a fellow member may be threatened, then all else is forgotten. He knows full well what his priorities are, and defence of his friends is top of the list.

One sunny August day, when we were on holiday in Wiltshire, I was sitting on the grass in the middle of a large old stable yard cleaning the harness. Bobbin was stretched out beside me in the sun, enjoying this moment of relaxation. Some chickens were scratching around at the other side of the courtyard, and after a while they began to move in our direction. As they began to scratch nearer to where Bobbin was lying, he got up and moved closer to me. Still they came nearer, and again he moved closer. On came the fearless fowl, until at last they were scratching all around us, and Bobbin was positively huddled up against me. He was beginning to look quite miserable at this siege, and suddenly I felt that we had had enough of these brazen birds. Brandishing my sponge at them I shouted, "Go away! Go away, and leave us alone!"

Instantly Bobbin picked up the note of anger in my voice. He leapt up, and with totally altered demeanour he charged at the hens and barked until they had fluttered off to a safe distance. Then, having satisfactorily secured our safety with regard to predatory poultry, he resumed his original sun spot and lay down to continue his sun-bathing undisturbed.

On one occasion, too, Bobbin overcame his terror and actually risked chasing a flock of sheep; and once again, his courage was motivated by desire to protect his own. It was after the great storm in October 1987, when the fence separating the farmer's sheep from Cookie's field was damaged, and every day a score or two of sheep would invade the paddock and devour his grass. This was particularly annoying as the grass was intended as fodder for December, to postpone the expense of feeding hay for as long as possible. Poor Alf was busy enough repairing other damage on the farm but eventually after a couple of weeks, to my relief, he patched up the fence. Good! I thought. Still a little grass left: and no more sheep!

But it wasn't so easy. The next day these determined creatures had broken through again, and I felt exasperated. I wanted them out; and, half-wondering whether it was a wise thing to do, I called Bobbin and said, "See them off! Get those sheep out of here!" Although he had tolerated their presence without demur for over a fortnight, Bobbin immediately understood. He tore off down the field, and barking in a warning tone, he rounded up the sheep and drove them back down towards the strip of trees that separated Cookie's field from Alf's. My heart was beating fast: suppose he didn't stop when they had gone? Had I, in a moment of frustration and anger, undone a life-time's training?

Of course, I need not have worried. Once the last sheep was out of our field, Bobbin turned round and raced back up the hill, eager to tell me all about how he had got rid of them. And he has never chased any sheep since then.

Chapter 11: Rabbits and Squirrels - Fair Game

Since his early lessons, Bobbin's behaviour towards farm animals has always been exemplary. But he instinctively knows that wild animals are in a different category. These he can chase, as furiously as he likes; but as he has discovered, with very little chance of success. Although his chief pleasure seems always to be the fun of the chase, rather than the prospect of a snack, even in this Bobbin is often thwarted. Most of the animals he encounters not only refuse to stop and play, but also frequently avail themselves of some unfair advantage to win the game before it has really started.

Deer in plenty have shown Bobbin their heels. When he was in the first flush of zealous youth, he did his utmost to give them a run for their money, tearing flat out across a twenty acre stubble field in pursuit of a running deer. He soon learnt, from the constant frustration of even his best endeavours, that this was an expense of energy which simply was not worth the effort. By the time he was eighteen months old, he had arrived at a compromise to satisfy his honour. He would rush a few paces when he came across a deer, and then he would suddenly turn aside, as though he had discovered something far more interesting, and allow the deer to escape while he was otherwise engaged. He would watch it go, standing with forepaw raised and ears quivering, as if to emphasise the point that *he* had seen it off, and it had better not come back, or he would be waiting ....

In spite of the fact that he was so near to the ground, and I had a far greater vantage point up on horseback, he was always the first to know when a roe deer was lurking in the bushes, or blending into the blue haze of dusk far away across a field. Thanks to his senses, I have many times had the opportunity to stop and gaze on a lovely scene which I would have missed if I had only had my own dull wits to rely on: a group of deer, their long necks bent gracefully in the twilight over the new young corn, or a handsome stag with antlers upraised, motionless in the undergrowth.

For Love of a Dog

Cats, squirrels and rabbits, however, have remained a challenge which must never be ignored. Even as I write these well-known magic words, Bobbin, sleeping peacefully at my feet, begins suddenly to twitch his paws and make little running movements in his sleep as though once again he is re-living, through a dream, one of those thrilling chases down the garden or across the field.

Just as his reactions at night reflect his different perceptions of different types of creature, so too the manner in which he conducts the chase varies according to the nature of his quarry. There is something very deep-rooted about his dislike of cats, and his whole demeanour makes it clear that a cat is an abomination not to be tolerated anywhere, but least of all on his territory. His hunting of rabbits is characterised by silence and speed, but his pursuit of a cat is accompanied by vociferous barking, which clearly denotes a special sense of outrage at the very presence of the feline species. When he sees off a cat, his tail is up, indicating assertiveness; when he hunts a rabbit, his tail is down to give him as much disguise as possible. When he is in pursuit of enemy cat, his hackles are raised and he seems larger and more muscular than usual. But when he chases a rabbit he adopts the slinky profile of the predator.

Bobbin has my whole-hearted sympathy in the matter of cats. They have offensive habits of needlessly decimating the valuable bird and lizard population in my garden, and I am usually as sorry as Bobbin is when the nifty creature springs slyly up a tree, or on to the roof of the shed to peer down at us and add insult to injury. I have been known to lend Bobbin my support in these circumstances with the employment of a judiciously flung cup of water .... and then of course I congratulate Bobbin on getting rid of the unwelcome intruder, and he can return proudly to his duties as watchman with the feeling of a job well done.

Rabbits and squirrels are a different proposition. For a start, these may be encountered anywhere. When he is out and about, a Jack Russell's nose is constantly busy sorting out the scents both of members of his own species who have passed that way (potential allies or potential foes) and also of other creatures (potential game). With all his senses equally alert to any faint rustle in the undergrowth, or the flicker of movement somewhere in the grass, it is never long before he detects some likely quarry.

You will see many beautiful and wonderful sights if you watch a dog's behaviour closely; but one which I can never tire of watching is that moment of transformation when the prey is spotted. Bobbin has been trotting along, quietly engrossed in registering the significance of the pieces of evidence he finds about what has been happening along this path. He is relaxed, and enjoying the walk. Suddenly, from somewhere under that beech tree he hears the scurry of a squirrel in the leaf mould. In a split second, his whole bearing alters. Every muscle in his body becomes taut as a bowstring; he seems to grow two inches taller, his ears and tail are raised as though he would flaunt them as banners to the fray, and with a spring that would do credit to an Olympic gymnast, he is off. Straight as an arrow he races towards his target, and as he goes, he instinctively flattens his ears and lowers his tail, thus offering the least wind resistance and releasing maximum speed. In these bursts of acceleration he appears to achieve incredible speeds: but even so, the squirrel always seems to have time enough to sit up on its haunches, fling Bobbin a tantalising glance as if trying to work out his ETA, give a coy whisk of its tail and execute a few pirouetting bounces before at the last moment leaping sideways and vanishing up a tree.

Bobbin puts all his very best endeavours into that sprint, but he still gets out-manoeuvred time after time. The last thing I want is for him to catch any kind of creature, but I do wish those squirrels would not look quite so smug as they skip lightly up a handy tree and scamper off with scarcely a backward smirk.

Rabbits are a bit more hopeful: but here, too, Bobbin seems always to be at a disadvantage. They have that irritating knack of disappearing down burrows where he is forbidden to follow. One September evening, however, he had the chance of a lifetime to achieve his ambition with the merest snap of his jaws ....

We were riding along a familiar path between the river and a pasture field - a place where Bobbin invariably looks out for rabbits, and generally manages to scare at least one or two back into their burrows. We were brought to a standstill by the sight of a rather odd-looking creature crossing the path in front of us. At first, in the half light, I couldn't make out what it was; then as we drew nearer I realised that it was a black cat with a large live rabbit dangling limply from its mouth. It was clearly about to take it home across the fields to the farm house. Moved by a sudden compassion for the rabbit, I dismounted, and standing in front of the cat, I told it to let it go.

Too late did I realise that, as the cat-and-rabbit was just in front of my boots, so the Jack-Russell-without-rabbit was just behind them. As the cat dropped its prey, the rabbit shot between my feet straight towards the jaws of an even fiercer potential predator. "Leave it, Bobbin!" I yelled. To my intense relief, Bobbin stepped back and just let it pass. I must admit that I was not a little impressed that a habit of trained obedience could overcome even such a basic instinct.

Watching Bobbin in hot pursuit has always been to me a double-edged pleasure. On the one hand, I long, for his sake, to see him for once achieve his goal, while on the other I dread the thought of watching an innocent creature writhing in hopeless misery. But the sight of that concentration of energy, single-minded and mighty-muscled in the chase, is to me every bit as thrilling and beautiful as it is to many people to watch the powerful movements of a cheetah hunting on the screens of their television sets.... and cheetahs don't come racing back to you with shining eyes and an expression of exhilaration and joy that says, "Oh, what *fun*! Didn't I do well? You don't know what you missed! I just so very nearly caught it!"

Bobbin finally did catch a rabbit. One fine spring morning we had wandered far into the Dorset downs, and Bobbin was silhouetted on an ancient barrow about a hundred yards off when I heard a hideous squealing. Even at that distance, it was plain to see that it was a large, old rabbit, infested with myxomatosis. Bobbin was holding it by the scruff of its neck and thumping it vigorously up and down while it screamed piteously. I considered for a moment: it was probably half dead by now, and certainly unlikely to survive if it was released. Even if it did survive the shock, its death from disease would be slow and painful. I decided to let nature take its natural - and as I believed, kinder - course: and I was wiser for the experience. I just stood and watched, trying to block my ears until the screaming stopped. When eventually there was silence, I called Bobbin back to me: and that was when the trouble really started. Every one of the old rabbit's multitudinous population of fleas had seized its chance and skipped speedily on to this more hopeful source of survival.

As we began to hurry back towards the car, Bobbin was stopping every few yards to throw himself desperately on the ground. Each time he paused to roll, I tried to grab hold of a handful of little black fleas. As soon as we were in the car, we set off as fast as we possibly could for home. Several times I had to stop to retrieve the now demented dog from some corner of the vehicle, and snatch another dozen or so fleas and throw them out of the window. When at last we were home, Bobbin went straight into the bath: a very potent medicated bath, which exterminated the plague of parasites without delay. I knew now that my idea of letting nature take its course was not an experiment we should wish to repeat.

For Love of a Dog

Even if it had been kinder for the rabbit, for Bobbin, his moment of triumph had very quickly turned to near disaster.

It is always a joy to watch Bobbin's supreme speed in the chase; but one day this simple pleasure was touched by sickening panic. We had stopped by a field in Dorset's lovely Marshwood Vale to admire the view and get a breath of fresh air. As I wandered through the open gate, Bobbin was already ahead of me. For a moment he stood quivering, his nose pointing at something I could not see. Then like a streak of lightning he tore off down the field.

There is something so magical about witnessing this miraculous burst of acceleration, that at first I stood there feeling as excited as he was. I could not make out what he was chasing, but something low to the ground was fleeing rather bumpily towards the hedge. To my delight I saw that Bobbin was gaining on it. I couldn't help inwardly cheering him on. Well done, Bobbin! I thought, smiling to myself. What a splendid chase! As the distance between them closed, I was becoming as thrilled as he was.

For Love of a Dog

He had narrowed the gap to only a few feet when I suddenly realised what it was - a badger! My delight at seeing a badger in broad daylight was short-lived. Suddenly I foresaw what could happen if Bobbin drew any closer: one swipe of that powerful forepaw would certainly do untold damage. I began to run too, and to shout, wishing I had called him back sooner.

At that moment the badger shot into the hedge. Hearing my call Bobbin stopped. For a few seconds he hesitated. Then, to my great relief, triumphant at having seen off the foe, he turned and came racing obediently back to tell me all about it. Once again I had learned a lesson. In future, when occasionally we met a badger in the woods, pursuit was firmly forbidden. This wild animal was definitely to be off limits.

But there is one animal whom Bobbin has always regarded as a natural adversary, and worthy of his most determined efforts: an equal yet an intolerable foe - the fox. For many years we have had a fox living near the end of our garden and night after night Bobbin listens, alert for that moment when it makes its regular journey across the lawn, round the side of the house, and off into the darkness to hunt. Through Bobbin's faultless senses of hearing and smell, I have been able to plot the exact timetable of the fox's movements, and to watch his comings and goings. Now that Bobbin is older, and his hearing is less sharp, he relies even more on his sense of smell, and follows the fresh scent of the fox up and down the garden when he makes his nightly excursions outside, so that I can see exactly which route our visitor has taken.

But for many years the highlight of Bobbin's day was his nocturnal hunting of the fox in the pony's field. Each night we would go to feed Cookie at about half past nine, and if the night was fine we would sit up there with the pony, gazing down the moon-bathed hill and across the moonlit valley. For the pony, this was a time of contented munching and companionship; for me it was a time of peaceful reflection and contentment. But for Bobbin, this was the moment when his whole being was alert in anticipation. Foxes are creatures of regular habit, and each night at two minutes past ten our vixen would sneak through the hedge from the lane, and slink down the field to the woods.

This was the time above all other when Bobbin could be most truly himself. He would sit bolt upright, with his friends beside him by the stable door, eyes focused on the blackness beyond. Every muscle taut, ears pricked, tensely ready for the prospective chase, he was oblivious to all else as he waited for the first hint of a movement. Then, faster than an arrow from a bow, he would tear down through the darkness of the field, barking as though he would waken the dead from their slumbers. Dog and invisible fox would vanish in an instant into the tangled undergrowth of the steep banks below, and for a few minutes all would be silent. Then, just when I was beginning to get anxious, a small pale shape would emerge, puffing valiantly back up the hill, looking for all the world as proud as if he had personally vanquished all the foxes till kingdom come.

I am quite sure he never came close enough to nip a tail; but the exhilaration and joy which his endeavours brought him meant that he returned home each night tired, happy, and ready for a well-earned, dreamful sleep.

Chapter 12: Best Friends

Bobbin was only eight weeks old when first I took him to meet Cookie. Carefully I lifted him in my arms, and held him up to meet the horse who for twelve years was to be his best friend. With a gentleness that barely struck me at the time, the pony stretched out his long nose to investigate this tiny bundle of fur, and horse and dog sniffed each other's nostrils with infinite tenderness. Those few seconds were the beginning of as deep and loyal a friendship as you could find anywhere. From that moment their devotion was without reserve.

The bond between horse and dog was something which arose spontaneously; neither Cookie nor Bobbin ever needed any prompting in the matter of tolerance or good manners. And as their mutual respect and comradeship grew and deepened over the years they spent together, every outing was enriched by the friendship and trust which they shared.

Cookie had been with me for six years now, and had proved himself to be a thoroughly trustworthy and kind pony. Being a true Welsh Cob, there were times when he could show all the spark and fire of his breeding; but I knew that, when it really mattered, he would always be dependable. So when first I carried my tiny new puppy up to the field, and held him up for Cookie to sniff in my arms, it did not occur to me to have any doubts about Cookie's reaction. I simply wanted Cookie to share with me the delight that I felt in this small newcomer to our family. And he did: more than I could ever have imagined.

It was a few weeks before Bobbin could begin to accompany us on our rides. First he must have his vaccinations, and then the wintry weather meant that we had to choose his days carefully. But once he was strong enough to come with us, we had to work out how best he could share in our outings. We tried various methods: his very first experiences of horsemanship involved being carried snugly inside my coat. But this did not last long: he soon outgrew my jacket pocket. It was impossible to fit enough of him in, and he was in constant danger of falling out. Next we tried the saddlebag; but his enthusiasm for wriggling up to explore this interesting viewpoint rendered this too risky as well.

At last, we found a solution. Bobbin was strapped into a dog harness, which was easier to keep hold of than a collar. In this way, he could perch in front of me on the pommel of the saddle, and cuddle into my jacket to keep warm. Cookie never for a moment demurred at having a set of four sharp-clawed feet scrambling from time to time on and off his withers; and, for his part, Bobbin took to this form of transport as though it was exactly what he had hoped for when he had made his plans for the world.

Soon it became surprisingly easy and comfortable. But apparently it didn't seem quite so natural to other people. "Full marks for novelty!" was the reaction of one gentleman; and almost everyone we met made a comment of one sort or another. It was entertaining, when we saw walkers approaching, to try to guess what sort of people they were, and what they would say, and I started making a collection of some of their remarks. I found that almost invariably they would fall into one of three categories: miserable, cheerful, or imaginative.

The miserable and cheerful were fairly equally balanced. The 'miserable' ones would see us coming, and hail us as we approached with some greeting such as, "What a lazy dog!" or "Hasn't he got legs of his own?" "You ought to make him walk. He'll get fat."

Sometimes these priggish reproaches would irritate me and make me want to reply, "Your legs are five times as long as his. Would you like to try keeping pace with us as we trot out over the downs for the next two miles?"

The cheerful ones, on the other hand, would greet us with a smile. "What a lucky dog! Isn't he having a nice ride!" or, "What a lovely way to travel! He looks so happy up there!"

And he did. Bobbin riding his horse was in his element. This was when life was at its best, on an adventure with his two best friends: he exuded happiness and pride. He looked and felt superior to all the world - which of course, to my way of thinking, he always has been.

Some would utter expressions of admiration or surprise. "What a clever dog! How does he stay on?" "Well! I've never seen that before! Now I've seen everything!" "A dog riding a horse!! Just wait till I tell my daughter about this!" Reactions such as these were far more welcome.

There were fewer of the more inventive comments, and I made a special note of these. "That dog's no fool! He's really got you where he wants you."
"Shouldn't he be wearing a hard hat too?" "Hasn't he got any stirrups?" "Why don't you get him a pony of his own?"

Bobbin's powers of balance were remarkable. Once his muscles were fully developed, he was perfectly able to maintain his own position - front feet on Cookie's neck, hind feet on the pommel - without any support; but I always made sure that my hands were safely on either side of him, ready to steady him if the pony spooked. We had many narrow escapes, and several scary moments; but only once did Bobbin fall from his perch, when Cookie swerved violently at some imagined terror, and neither of us was prepared. I was horrified, and Cookie looked very chastened when he realised what he had done to his best friend. But Bobbin, being both relaxed and resilient, simply rolled over and leapt up with a brisk shake, ready to carry on again as if nothing had happened.

Mounting Cookie with Bobbin became something of an art. I have met dogs who were able to leap up to the saddle from the ground, or an eminence such as a log. Bobbin never mastered this knack, so I always had to dismount to pick him up. The procedure was thus:

1 Lift Bobbin up on to the pommel of the saddle;
2 Place my hands on Cookie's withers either side of Bobbin
3 Spring into the saddle behind him, taking care not to dislodge him as I land in the seat.

This was quite straightforward. But one day I took a bigger leap than usual, and somehow both of us went sailing over the top to land in the road at the other side. Cookie, always reliable, stood like a rock, patiently looking down at us as we scrambled to our feet - no doubt thinking what fools we looked.

For Love of a Dog

Bobbin was so confident in the saddle that even when Cookie was upset by something, and it needed all my concentration to control him, it was still preferable to keep him close to me on the horse. Bobbin gave Cookie confidence, and had a calming effect on him: Cookie took his responsibility for his friend very seriously.

As long as they were together, pony and dog were happy. Wherever we went, they felt secure and were reassured by each other's company. If ever I had to leave Cookie unattended for a few minutes - tied up outside a shop, or for some similar reason - it was usually simplest to leave Bobbin *in situ* on the edge of the saddle. Then I knew that they both would be safe together: each would look after the other.

The degree of trust and cooperation which grew up between dog and horse was something very special, and it brought an extra dimension of closeness and camaraderie to all our excursions. If Bobbin got too far ahead, he would stop and wait for Cookie. If Bobbin was left behind, Cookie would pause and turn his head back to see if he was coming. In the early days, particularly if the going was hard or stony, it was usually Bobbin who would outstrip the pony, and would stand panting at a bend in the path, or rush impatiently back to us and off again, as if to say, "Do hurry up! Why are you being so *slow*? Can't you see I'm waiting for you!"

But when we got to a place where the ground was soft or grassy, a place where we could have a canter, then horse and dog would race side by side. Flying like the wind, each took all the greater delight in their speed for the company of the other, and many's the time they have run their own private Derby on some quiet stretch of downland turf. Often I would pull up the pony in order to let Bobbin 'win', aware that he was straining every muscle and needed more time to recover from his sprinting than the larger animal. Only rarely would he let me pick him up and give him a rest. Time and again, he would elude my embrace. Certain that he must be exhausted, I would repeatedly dismount and try to get hold of him, only to be foiled as he would dash off ahead of us once more.

Bobbin accompanied us on rides through the Surrey hills for hours on end. In spite of the pace required to keep up with his friends, he would still find time to race across the downs to investigate a rabbit warren, or to pursue a scampering squirrel in the woods. He made many friends, and had many a brief encounter with fellow dogs. He also developed a sound knowledge of the network of pathways of his territory. Even now, he could still lead me unerringly along the shortest route to home from any starting point within a wide radius.

Bobbin loved the freedom of our rides: it suited his independent spirit. He could look after himself. If he was thirsty, he had an innate skill for finding water. He knew that the larger beech trees may have little dips where rainwater collects, and if we were in woodland, he would sniff carefully round any likely-looking trunks. Once he found a place, he always remembered it, and would visit it time and again. But if we were in open country, he seemed able to smell water from a great distance. At times when he could not possibly have seen it from ground level, he would suddenly leave the path and make a beeline across a field to reach a water tank a hundred yards away. Here he would perform incredible feats of agility in order to reach the water: I have seen him pull himself up and hold on by his front paws even when the tank is raised up well above his height.

For Love of a Dog

Being carried was only a last resort of exhaustion. Although it was a necessity to which he submitted without complaint if we were doing any roadwork, at other times Bobbin's proud and independent spirit would vigorously resist offers of help. It was constantly surprising to see the resources of energy he seemed able to draw on when it would have been natural for him to be weary.

There is a theory that dogs have an instinctive ability to pace themselves when travelling distances, and certainly Bobbin's behaviour seemed to bear out this theory. No matter how far we had been, or how tired he appeared to be, on the final downhill stretch of our journey home, Bobbin seemed always to gain a new lease of life, as if he were tapping a hidden reserve of energy. Suddenly he would break into a run, and invariably search about for a stick. He would toss it in the air, pursue it and pounce on it, and then with hideous growls set about shaking it ferociously. He would repeat this performance two or three times and then, just as suddenly, he would lose interest, as though he had simply wanted to say, "There! You see? I'm not tired after all! I've still got the energy to play my game!"

One hot August afternoon the pony lost a shoe, and we were obliged to leave him for the night in a village about fourteen miles from home. Bobbin and I had to make our way home on foot. Bobbin had already travelled fourteen miles in the heat; the return journey would mean another fourteen miles, and involve crossing two ranges of hills ... how would he cope?

We took it gently, and made the most of every opportunity to idle by a refreshing stream, or dawdle on a shady bank to gather wild strawberries. Several times I insisted that Bobbin submit to a little 'carry', and we eventually completed the journey in about five hours. By the time we reached the top of our hill, I was completely exhausted.

"Nearly there!" I said to Bobbin, thinking longingly of a comfortable chair and a cup of tea. To my astonishment, Bobbin suddenly raced off into the undergrowth. A moment later, he emerged with a stick, which he proceeded to toss and chase with all his usual energy and delight until we got back to the field.

In his later years, Bobbin had to put up with being carried more and more often, and sometimes against his wishes. But it was easy to tell when he needed a lift; if he still had some energy left, he wouldn't let me touch him. And once he had fully recovered, I had no option but to let him down before he could wrench himself free and take a dangerous flying leap.

Pony and dog were sensitive to each other's every mood, and shared each other's delights. Bobbin would be happy for hours, just mooching about in the field, or grazing somewhere in the middle of the countryside with Cookie. When Bobbin saw Cookie eating grass at some wayside halt, he would try nibbling a few blades himself; when Cookie was given a carrot, Bobbin, who normally eschews everything vegetarian, would munch happily on his own share; and when Cookie was given his feed of pony nuts, Bobbin would put his head in the bucket and share the meal. But if I tried giving Bobbin any carrots or pony nuts when he was at home, he would turn up his nose and look scathingly at me as if I was trying to play a trick on him - like those maddening children who will eat fish fingers at Samantha's house, but never touch them when they are at home.

One thing troubled them both equally: sneezing. Why this should have been so alarming, I could never understand. Neither horse nor dog reacted so violently to any similar sudden noise, such as a cough or a bark. It was as if the sneeze of one was in some primeval way shared by the other. If Bobbin sneezed when he was trotting ahead of us along the track, Cookie would nearly jump out of his skin, and I could feel the shiver of his legs beneath me. When Cookie sneezed, Bobbin would stop abruptly in his tracks, turn and look as startled as if the sky had fallen. Then, as if he had suddenly decided that the sneeze had been some kind of hilarious joke, he would turn and race back to us, jump up at Cookie, do a wild fandango round and round us and hare off up the hill again as if the fun of it had given him a new zest for life.

The times that Bobbin spent with his friend Cookie were beyond a doubt some of the happiest and most complete of his life. He delighted in the opportunities for adventure afforded by his unchallenged lordship over the two acres of field and woodland where Cookie lived, and he basked in the quiet companionship of his friend. He enjoyed the days when the farrier would come, and he would dart perilously in and out of Cookie's feet, snatching delicious scraps of hoof trimming to devour with intense relish. He loved to track down a mouse in Cookie's stable, and would spend hours standing motionless and watchful over a heap of straw, in an unshakeable belief that eventually his quarry would emerge. The fact that this never happened did not deter him. He is an optimistic dog; and after all, he has found so many times that steadfast faith is, in the end, rewarded.

To Bobbin, Cookie's stable was his home from home. Here he was in the open air where he loves best to be, with both his dearest friends, on his own undisputed territory, and with plenty to do. And if he was tired, or chilly - or sometimes, I think, just for fun - he would make himself a cosy bed, scuffing up the straw and turning round and round until he was snuggled deep into a comforting nest.

I have often thought that the bed that he made for himself in Cookie's stable gave him greater comfort and satisfaction than any of the many baskets and sheepskin rugs I have given him at home. In many ways, for Bobbin, the home he shared for so many hours with his friend, was where, if he could have, he would have liked to stay forever.

Chapter 13: A Friend in Need

Pony and dog worked together in wordless harmony; wherever we were, they were a team. When we were at home in the field, they would stand contentedly side by side for hours. When we were out riding, Bobbin would trot along at Cookie's heels, or so close beside him that often, where the path was narrow, I would be fearful for his safety. One false step could have done unimaginable damage. But Cookie took constant pains to safeguard his friend. Only once, when in an excess of enthusiasm to get in front, he shot right under Cookie's feet as he was cantering, did Cookie accidentally catch him lightly with his hoof; and the only harm was a momentary deflation of Bobbin's *joie de vivre*.

Each had his own special strengths, and each knew instinctively how he could help the other, when his help was needed. If Bobbin was tired, Cookie would stop and wait for him. If Cookie was nervous, Bobbin would go on ahead and encourage him. When Bobbin was frightened, Cookie would put up with the violent struggles of his friend as I strove to keep him steady on the saddle, and continue calmly at a smooth pace, as though he knew very well that I literally had my hands full, and his job was to get us both home safely.

One summer evening we had been out for a peaceful ride in the late evening sun. We had just reached the top of the downs about a mile from home, when without warning a hot air balloon suddenly appeared above us. Bobbin was terrified; perhaps the apparition seemed to him to be a monstrous bird of prey, and it was very close. Before I could dismount and catch him, he had bolted at top speed along the path and was heading down the hill. Panic-stricken, he was for once deaf to my calls as he tore off out of sight. Would he stop at the field? There was no one there to reassure him. Or would he, gripped by the overwhelming desire to escape, carry on running down towards the road?

It was an agonising dilemma, and my loyalties were painfully divided. Cookie was just recovering from a bout of lameness, and was supposed to be taking only gentle exercise at a walk; and between us and the field was a downhill tarmac lane which was slippery at the best of times. It would be madness to put Cookie at risk by allowing him to go too fast for his own good; and yet Bobbin's safety might depend on our being able to reach him before he had an accident. I did not know what to do. So I put my trust in Cookie, and gave him his head.

Fortunately, Cookie had no anxieties about hot air balloons; but he seemed instinctively to understand what was at stake - the safety of his friend. As I relaxed the reins and hesitantly pressed him forward with my leg, he responded by breaking into his briskest trot, and set off as fast as he could to try to catch up with his terrified friend. To overtake him was out of the question: even on level going Bobbin could often out-run Cookie. Downhill there was no contest.

Somehow, we tore down that hill at a speed I could not afterwards bear to think of, yet still only just managing to keep Bobbin in sight. At last, at a bend in the road just before the field, Bobbin paused for breath, and leaping from the saddle without halting Cookie, I managed to catch hold of him. Thanks to Cookie, we had caught up with him in time. Cookie had saved the day - and his friend.

More frequently, it was Bobbin who protected Cookie. Instinctively he knew that his duty was to guard his two friends; and although he always enjoyed foraging in the stable or hunting in the field, often while I was grooming or mucking out he would instead remain at his self-appointed post - on guard outside the gate. He would sit bolt upright, ears pricked, looking up and down the road, visibly tensing at any sign of movement.

If he spied strangers coming, he would lose no time in letting them know whose territory they were approaching. Taking up an uncompromising position in the centre of the lane, he would stare at them hard, making sure that they could not pass unchallenged.

If they began to get too close, or if they looked in any way suspicious, then he would adopt more assertive methods, and begin barking in a manner which was clearly designed to give warning of intruders. He was never aggressive; he would simply keep a close eye on things, and stand his ground until the threat had passed. If a stranger attempted to patronise him by calling him a 'dear doggie' or - oh horrors! - trying to *pat* him, he would have none of it. Dodging skillfully just out of reach, he would become even more suspicious. Only if I greeted the strangers as friends, did he know that he could go off duty. But he never relaxed his determination to keep his distance.

Bobbin has never behaved aggressively to anyone; he simply knows that he must take care of his friends. So Cookie and I could go anywhere with a feeling of confidence, knowing that we had a protector with very sharp teeth, should the need ever arise. Fortunately it never did.

But Bobbin's fearlessness and courage helped us out of many another quandary.

Apart from hot air balloons, there were few things which we encountered on our rides that held any terror for Bobbin. Cookie, on the other hand, would sometimes be unaccountably terrified of walking past a log or a flapping leaf. On these occasions, Bobbin came into his own. He seemed to sense what was scaring the pony. He would go on ahead, go up to the *bête noire*, sniff it, and glance encouragingly back at Cookie. Then, with a nonchalant shrug, he would romp on up the track, as if urging his friend to follow. Bobbin had vanquished the foe, and Cookie would walk on by with scarcely a second look.

During the winter, when I was at work during the day, we often had to ride out in the dark. The paths were wide, traffic-free and familiar, and it was perfectly safe because there were always two pairs of eyes better than my own to rely on. Cookie would spot the movement of a living creature as soon as Bobbin could, but it was from Bobbin's reactions that I could tell whether we were about to meet an animal or another human being. If it was a fox, Bobbin would be hell-bent on chasing it; but if it was a human, he would stand his ground and begin one of his low, throaty, threatening growls, and I could feel the hairs on his spine begin to bristle.

Bobbin's boldness gave us confidence in many situations. But his greatest strength lay in his courage and initiative in protecting us from cattle. Time after time he saved Cookie from imaginary, and me from very real danger. Cookie was terrified of cattle. He hated the way they would come galumphing in a herd to peer inquisitively at us as we rode by. Even to pass by a field of young steers was risky; to attempt to ride through the field was downright dangerous. I had tried in vain to help Cookie to overcome his fears, and to become accustomed to cattle, and I had repeatedly failed. However safe the distance, these attempts had always ended with Cookie bolting at tremendous speed in the opposite direction - regardless of any obstacles, such as trees, which might be in his path. After a while I gave up the unequal struggle; discretion seemed definitely to be the better part of valour.

But with Bobbin on our side, the problem was soon solved. Cookie remained panic-stricken at the sight of bovines of any description; but Bobbin was not. This, he saw at once, was an opportunity for his assistance. Certainly I never showed him what to do: I would not have known how.

One day, on our way home, we unexpectedly had to pass a field of bullocks which had just been turned out. It was getting dark. To change our route would mean a back-tracking detour of two or three miles: to continue was inviting trouble. The path was narrow, with a barbed wire fence on one side and a wood on the other. If Cookie bolted now, I could be knocked off on a tree and he would risk injuring himself on the barbed wire. Suddenly the bullocks saw us, and their leader let out a roar. Cookie stiffened in fright: and the bullocks began to move, with that peculiar sort of sideways gallop, towards us.

Bobbin looked up. For a moment he paused; he glanced at Cookie and then at me, and in an instant he seemed to sum up the situation. Without hesitation, he shot under the fence and made a beeline towards the cattle. The bullocks stopped in their tracks; and as if he had done this hundreds of times before, Bobbin instantly followed up his advantage. Keeping his eyes firmly fixed on the menacing beasts, with his ears on full alert, he continued his advance towards them. Slowly they began to back away; and as they did so, Bobbin made quite sure that he had them all covered.

He began to run up and down, zigzagging from left to right and back again; and all the time he was pushing them further away from me and Cookie. If one of them tried to break out and make a rush towards us, Bobbin was there. He seemed to have eyes on all of them at once: whatever any of the cattle did, he was ready. Although they were spread out over at least a hundred yards of field, not one of them was allowed to break out of line or advance a step towards us.

Cookie was quick to take advantage of the retreat. As soon as he saw the cattle backing away, he began to relax, and trotted on along the path without attempting to bolt. His confidence had returned, and in a few moments the danger was behind us: we were safely past the field. And now I realised that throughout all his manoeuvring, Bobbin had had one eye on us. As we reached the end of the field in safety, he glanced quickly over his shoulder at us, and I could see his tail and ears relax. Then, with one final sally and a bark of triumph at the chastened kine, he turned tail and raced as fast as his legs would carry him across the field and back under the fence. He was out of breath, but his eyes were shining; and there was no mistaking the expression of satisfaction on his face which said, "There! That showed them! Now let's get home for dinner!"

After that first occasion, I lost count of the number of times Bobbin got us out of a similar impasse. But I never ceased to marvel at the quickness with which he saw our difficulty, or at the bravery with which such a small dog - who was scared of sheep - would out-face a bullying herd of cattle, in order that his friends could pass by in safety.

But Cookie, too, had his chance to save his friend. One frosty winter's day, when we were far from home, a terrible thing happened to Bobbin; and on this occasion, Cookie truly did his very utmost in what seemed at the time to be a matter of life and death.

It was just before Christmas, and we had gone down to Wiltshire to stay a few days with our old friend Gill, to enjoy the riding on the open grassland of Martin Down. We had often visited this area in the summer, and by now we knew the beautiful countryside almost as well as we knew our own Surrey hills. A little while after we arrived, I decided to take Cookie out for an hour or so to stretch his legs before settling him down for the night. Because he might be frisky with excitement at this change of surroundings, it seemed better for that first ride to go on our own; and Gill set off in a different direction on her new three-year-old, Thomas. But of course Bobbin came too: he was longing for a race over the smooth flat turf.

It was a peaceful ride, and in spite of the temptation of the wide open spaces, Cookie behaved impeccably. But as luck would have it, in trying to avoid each other, Gill and I both chose a similar route and met in the middle of the open downs. We stopped for a chat; and we were just about to go our separate ways home when the nightmare began. Bobbin was sitting quietly on the grass about six feet away, and the horses were standing side by side, apparently relaxed. In a split second it happened: Thomas's front hoof lashed out, there was a tiny squeal, a sharp crack, and then a sickening thud. I saw Bobbin fly through the air: and then, as he lay motionless on the ground, all I could see was blood.

It has to be said that everyone behaved very well in this crisis except for me. I froze in panic, and very quickly became almost hysterical. When I could bring myself to look at Bobbin again, there was absolutely no sign of life. A black despair swept through me, and at that moment I felt no hope for him at all.

Gill began to talk to me. "Give me the reins," she was saying, "You've got to get off. You must get down and go to Bobbin."

But I couldn't do it. I was paralysed by the thought of what I would find. "Give me the reins," said Gill. "You must get down and go to Bobbin." I don't know how many times she said the same words. I remember only her calm voice repeatedly telling me what I had to do, until at last I too saw that I must get off Cookie and go to Bobbin.

"You must pick him up," I heard Gill's voice saying again and again, but still I couldn't bear to touch him. I remembered that sickening crack, and could not imagine that under all that blood Bobbin might still be alive. "You've got to pick him up and get him on Cookie. You must pick him up."

I am not proud of my behaviour; if it hadn't been for Gill's presence of mind and calmness, I don't know what I should have done. I can still vividly recall that feeling of profound helplessness, despair, and shock. One minute there had been my dog, sitting up happily and enjoying a little rest; the next moment he was unconscious and in mortal danger. It was entirely thanks to Gill's voice persistently repeating clear, simple instructions that I managed eventually to lift up Bobbin's helpless form, and wrap him in my jacket. Now I had to get him up on Cookie.

This had been easy enough in the past when Bobbin was conscious. But dealing with a dead weight was entirely different. Now Bobbin was quite unable to help himself by clinging on. Twice, as I balanced him on the saddle, and tried to jump up after him, he slipped off again over the other side, and fell heavily to the ground. My despair grew deeper; and all the while, panic-stricken as I was, I was aware that if my hysteria infected Cookie, the situation could become even worse. But Cookie had more sense than I did. Through all my dithering, he stood like a rock and gave me all the help he could, until at last we were both on the saddle, and ready to begin the journey home.

As we turned and began to move, I realised with horror what lay ahead of us. We were over two miles from Gill's house - there was none nearer - and all across open countryside with no possibility of assistance. Keeping hold of an unconscious dog was going to need my full concentration: and I felt that every minute counted. I could scarcely see for tears, and with Bobbin cradled in my arms I had barely a finger spare to hold the reins.

For Love of a Dog

For the first quarter of a mile Cookie went steadily and slowly, as if he were giving me time to get as much in control as I could. Blood was pouring down into my boot, over the saddle and down his side, and although horses are by nature terrified of the smell of blood, and Cookie must in addition have sensed the numb terror in me, he kept calm and went quietly forward. Then I heard Gill's voice saying, "I think I saw him move. I think he's going to be all right." And, although I did not dare to believe it, I thought I could perhaps feel a little more give in the dog's limp body. He was beginning very slightly to stir.

Cookie felt it too; for suddenly he began to quicken his pace, and there was nothing I could do to hold him back. Within a few moments, he had accelerated into a flat out gallop.

Although this journey was by its nature alarming in so many ways - one trip or stumble now would make our problems almost beyond hope - I have to admit that that gallop was also one of the most amazingly exhilarating experiences of my life. I had never known Cookie to go so fast. Each time I thought he could not go any faster, he did. Time after time he accelerated until it truly felt as if we were flying. But never had he gone more smoothly or more surely. His feet flew over the turf, with never a slip or a spook. His feet were flying, but his back remained as steady as a rock. I didn't need the reins, even if I could have held them. I knew that I could put all my trust in Cookie. I simply cradled Bobbin in my arms until we got home, sooner than I could ever have imagined. Cookie was determined to do his utmost for his friend - and he did.

When we eventually reached the vet in Salisbury, half an hour away, it was clear that Bobbin was beginning to come round. Although he was severely concussed, he had had a very lucky escape. Thomas's hoof had caught him between his eye and his muzzle. He had lost the skin off his face, and a lot of blood; but miraculously, as it seemed, no bones were broken.

It was a week or so before Bobbin was back to his usual self again, and he appeared to be none the worse for his ordeal. Certainly, his love of horses was undiminished: he clearly had no idea what had hit him, and although since then I have felt considerably more anxious about

For Love of a Dog

Bobbin's equine encounters, he has continued to greet every new horse he meets with eager enthusiasm.

When I think now of that winter's day, I feel again the blind panic that gripped me. But most of all I remember the courageous behaviour of Bobbin's best friend, and Cookie's determined dash to take his dearest friend to safety.

Chapter 14: Travelling Dog

The friendship between Bobbin and Cookie was further strengthened by the longer periods of time which they spent together on holiday. Before Bobbin joined our team, Cookie and I used to set off on holiday together three or four times a year. This involved packing as much as possible into two saddlebags, making a few arrangements about where to stay, praying very hard that it wouldn't pour with rain, and then setting off to explore a new part of the countryside. The pony enjoyed it as much as I did: the fresh surroundings and different paths stimulated him - and he had none of the problems of trying to cram spare shoes and grooming kits into two small saddlebags. But now that Bobbin's luggage had to be fitted in too, the enterprise, always rather a logistical problem, began to become almost unmanageable.

Apart from the luggage, there were other obvious difficulties. It didn't need a genius to work out that a dog with legs only six inches high cannot be expected to follow a whole day's ride on foot; he would need to have rests quite regularly. And when we had a goal to reach, often our journeys would involve more roadwork than we would have chosen. We couldn't risk trying an unfamiliar bridle path when, at the end of a long day's ride, with our destination in sight, we might have to turn back because the bridle path was blocked by a fallen tree, or because it traversed a field of rampaging bullocks. Bobbin accepted the inevitability of being carried occasionally when we were on roads; but having to carry him for mile after mile was not much fun for any of us.

After our first holiday together, it was clear that something would have to change. Bobbin was heroic - too heroic: but I didn't want to wear him out. And I couldn't fit a tin of dog food into the saddlebag however hard I tried.

The solution was obvious: we would get a trap. That way, Bobbin could travel in style, and even lie down and have a little sleep if he wanted. Not only would we be able to take as many tins of dog food as we needed, but also his sheepskin travel bed. And so, six months later,

For Love of a Dog

Cookie had been broken to harness, the trap was in the field shelter, and I had learnt to drive. From then on, Bobbin's holidays were considerably more comfortable, and he began to be a seasoned travelling dog.

To ensure that Bobbin was safe in the trap, some adjustments had to be made to the design of the cart. Normally, this type of vehicle is open on both sides at the front, so that (very essential) in an emergency the driver can exit fast to reach the pony's head. We had the left-hand gap blocked in, so that Bobbin could not fall out on the traffic side. I clipped a short lead to the rein-guard, so that when necessary he could be secured within the vehicle; but this, too could present problems. If the cart tipped over in an accident, Bobbin would be unable to get free. If there was trouble, and we had to bale out quickly, it would take precious seconds to unclip the lead. It was always a dilemma; but usually it seemed safer to leave Bobbin free so that he could make his own escape, if ever the need arose.

Bobbin relished these holidays. As soon as he saw me beginning to pack a bag, he would sit by it, and refuse to move unless it was with the luggage; and when he saw that we were going with Cookie, his excitement knew no bounds. Here was another chance for big adventures, for following fresh trails, for making new friends! And most important, he could spend day after day in the company of his best friend.

One of Bobbin's greatest loves is a horsebox. As the North Downs countryside near our home is very hilly and hard work for the beginning of a holiday, it often proved better to cover the first few miles in a horsebox, and then to set off from some easier territory. At the start of each holiday, Bobbin would stand by the field gate and watch, trembling with anticipation, for Mr. Legg's lorry to rumble up the narrow lane. The moment the ramp was lowered, he would be inside, eagerly investigating the elusive smells among the straw. His friend was not always so keen; he had had a bad experience some time in the past, and for several years it had been acutely difficult to lure Cookie into a horsebox. But once again, it was Bobbin who provided the solution to this problem.

It was at the beginning of one of our earliest holidays, and Bobbin could scarcely contain his impatience to be off. Quivering with excitement, he watched as Cookie was led up towards the ramp. Then, to his amazement, he saw him stop still, and refuse to take another step.

Bobbin could hardly believe his eyes. Two or three times we led Cookie round, and tried again, while Bobbin watched with increasing consternation and amazement. Then, suddenly, he seemed to make up his mind. With a flourish of his tail, he bounced up to Cookie, charged up the ramp into the box and turned round to face his friend. Half crouching, with eyes shining and wagging tail, he looked Cookie in the eye, and began to bark playfully.
"Come on!" he was saying, "It's all right! It's fun in here! Come on, and let's get going on our holiday!"
This encouragement from his trusted friend was all Cookie needed. Without so much as a sideways look, he walked straight up the ramp and settled down to munch his hay.

From that day on, there was seldom any trouble with boxing Cookie. He began to enjoy his outings as much as Bobbin did; and if ever he seemed to be having any second thoughts about leaving his field, we just sent Bobbin in, and Cookie would quickly follow. If his friend said it was all right, then he wasn't going to be left out. Wherever Bobbin went, Cookie was happy to follow.

Wherever we went, wherever we slept, during these weeks, the trap was home for Bobbin. In his spare moments, he would stretch out in the shade beneath it for a doze, or sit proudly on guard beside it.

On these holidays, too, Bobbin was a vital member of our team. It wasn't always possible to plan in advance where we would stay for the night: that was part of the adventure. Sometimes we could plan to stay with a friend; on other days we would have to find somewhere wherever we happened to be. Cookie always had to be the priority; the essential thing was to find a safe field for him for the night. Bobbin and I could make do. Sometimes we would be lucky and find a friendly farm that would put us up for the night, and sometimes Bobbin and I would spend the night in a hay barn or pitch our tent in a field. I always felt safe if Bobbin was there: I knew well that his eyes and ears, and his instinct for differentiating friend from foe, or scenting a danger long before I had any inkling of it, were the best protection I could have. I could fall asleep anywhere without qualms as long as I knew that Bobbin was at my side.

One night, however, while we were travelling in the depths of rural Hampshire, it seemed as if this arrangement had broken down, and for a few minutes I doubted the wisdom of being so relaxed about our plans. It was to be the first night in our new tent. But as we had been unable to find a suitable place to stay, I eventually decided, as darkness fell, to put up the tent in a stubble field well out of sight of the road. We appeared to be in the middle of nowhere, and we had not passed any houses for some miles. As I set about making camp, I felt reassured that I could see no house lights from our corner of the field, and no traffic was passing along the road. I just wished that our tent wasn't orange. We had some supper, zipped up the tent, and as the stars twinkled above us, fell soundly asleep.

In the middle of the night, something suddenly made me stir: a chill went down my spine, and in a second I was wide awake. It was pitch dark in the tent, but I could just make out the hands of my watch - it was a quarter to one in the morning. And unmistakably, outside the tent, something was shuffling quietly around. I lay paralysed with dread and listened. It was going round and round the tent. What could it be? A fox? An angry farmer? Some other lone wanderer of the night? I shivered as I thought of my predicament - why had I decided to camp alone in this remote field, so far from anywhere I knew? Why had it seemed such an advantage to be so far from any houses? Why wasn't Bobbin barking?

Anything would be better than to lie there, feeling trapped. With pulse pounding, I plucked up my courage and crawled to the entrance of the tent. With shaking hands I unzipped the closure and waited. Where was it? Then, with an overwhelming flood of astonishment and relief I saw not a fox, not a farmer, not some evil-minded villain, but my very own Bobbin, nose to the ground, intently tracking something, like Winnie the Pooh and the Heffalumps, round and round the tent. I couldn't see how he had got out; and I never discovered why. Perhaps he had just been making sure; or perhaps there had been a fox. At any rate, my adrenaline-rich anxiety state collapsed instantly into the relief of laughter. After that night, I always slept with Bobbin's lead slipped over my wrist, so that I knew he was there beside me. If there were to be any danger, then at least we would face it together.

Bobbin's life when we were travelling was a very busy one. He rarely lay down for a rest during the day; everything was new and exciting, and there was always something to watch or explore. He would stand, balancing precariously, with his feet up on the rein-guard, for mile after mile, gazing at the passing scenery, and keeping a look out for rabbits. Whenever we stopped for a break, he would lose no time in investigating his new surroundings, gathering information about what sort of dogs and people lived here. He would root about in the hedgerows, and sniff round gate posts, and of course always leave his message for any others who would come that way. When we stopped for the night, a whole new world of discovery began, and by the time we went to bed, he was exhausted.

Even then, he could not fully relax, but must always have at least half an ear on guard duty, so that he could be ready to warn his friends at the first sign of approaching danger. It was all right for me - thanks to Bobbin I could sleep peacefully; but for him it was more tiring than I had anticipated.

That first summer when we travelled with the trap was an idyllically hot and sunny one. Bobbin was about eighteen months old, and we set off from Somerset to make our way back to Dorking. Everywhere we went, Bobbin made new friends, and seemed to be having a wonderful time; but after a while the constant excitement began to take its toll. Apart from the continuous stimulation of his changing surroundings, it was a new thing for him simply to be awake all day. When I was working, he had developed his own routine of sleeping all day, scarcely stirring at lunch time, and then waking up ready for anything, with plenty of stored energy, when I came home and it was time to go out for a ride. Now, he was awake from five in the morning till eleven at night, with non-stop activity all day long. Being a conscientious dog, he couldn't allow himself to take time off. We were constantly entering new situations, and it was his responsibility to check them out for us. What was a holiday for me in fact meant that as a dutiful guard dog he had to do overtime, day after day.

The first intimation of his weariness came when we were about half way home. We had stopped for the night in a quiet village near Winchester, where we were entertained with luxurious hospitality by Fred and Audrey Burgess. We feasted on home grown tomatoes, and supped on rhubarb wine; and at last I put up the tent in their fairy-tale cottage garden beneath a prolific plum tree and fell soundly asleep. Bobbin fell soundly asleep too - very soundly. When it began to grow light the next morning, I went to fetch Cookie from the field. Bobbin didn't stir. I came back, and began to pack up our luggage and put it into the trap. Bobbin slept on. I made breakfast, and boiled the kettle for a cup of coffee. Still Bobbin lay, curled tightly into a ball, with his eyes fast shut. His whole curled body was saying quite clearly, "Go away. Leave me alone. Just leave me alone to sleep...."

Travelling as we were in the height of summer, it was important that we set off early, to avoid both traffic and hot sun. We had a drive of about twenty miles ahead of us today, and delay would lead to trouble later. We had to leave soon. Yet Bobbin remained deaf to my calls. At last everything else was ready: Cookie was harnessed, the luggage stowed. Only Bobbin and the tent remained. I had left him as long as possible.

After a final warning, I began to take down the tent. Still Bobbin did not stir. To my utter astonishment, he stayed where he was, curled up in his desperate bid for a day's rest, even after the whole tent had collapsed about him: and I still have a photograph of the orange tent lying on the ground with a round little hump in the middle ... a lump that was resolutely refusing to move.

He was so soundly asleep that I had to drag him out before finally rolling up the tent, but he had given me a warning. It was clear now that he needed more rest, and that he could not rest unless we all did. And so, for the next few days we tried to have some earlier nights, and to spend some more time relaxing during the day.

He soldiered valiantly on until a few days later, when we reached our last stop before home. We were to stay once again with our old friends Pat and Malc at Ewhurst. We had been there often before, and Bobbin knew their house as a home from home. As we pulled into their yard, he leapt out of the trap and went off, as I supposed, to hunt for a rabbit or find a drink of water. By the time Cookie was unharnessed, fed and turned out in the paddock, Bobbin had still not reappeared. Feeling a little concerned, I went to look for him. I searched in the kitchen, the living rooms and round the yard and paddocks. There was no sign of him. I began to be seriously worried. Could he have wandered back down the drive and into the road? Pat and Malc joined in the search. It was about an hour since we had arrived, and it was quite unlike Bobbin not to respond to my calls. We searched and searched again.

At last, when it was long past his supper time, we found him: stretched out underneath Pat's bed, and sound asleep. He had never been in her bedroom before; but he had sought out a place where he knew he would be least likely to be disturbed.

Nothing could wake him; it was clear now that seeing that at last we were all safely 'home' again, Bobbin had finally felt he could be off duty and catch up with his sleep. He was completely exhausted, and all we could do was wait till morning and hope he would recover. To my intense relief, after breakfast he began to show signs of life again. But we all agreed that he should not have to do any more travelling just yet. That day I finished the journey on my own with Cookie, and Pat very kindly brought Bobbin home in the car.

I learned a lesson from that first holiday. Bobbin was so courageous and enthusiastic, he always seemed ready for anything; but I realised now that even his energy had limits. From then on I tried to reward Bobbin's constant loyalty and watchfulness with a bit more consideration, making sure that we planned plenty of resting time into our schedule.

But those were happy times, too. There were days when Bobbin would spend hours hunting round the rabbit burrows of a different hedgerow, contented in the companionship of his equine friend. There were farmyards full of enticing smells to be explored, unfamiliar stables where mice could be stalked, and there were goats to make friends with. In the evenings, there were opportunities to make new conquests among the human species, and skillfully contrive to be offered roast beef or chicken nuggets by kind people who admired his native charm and eloquent looks - or simply couldn't resist his persuasive persistence. There were many days when he would stretch out luxuriously in the sun, for a spot of his favourite pastime, shifting into the shade of a convenient tree when he grew too hot. There were days, too, when he had to don his little blue mackintosh and weather the onset of a sudden shower with the rest of us, until we could seek shelter in an empty barn. And there were nights when, as the first frosts of autumn quivered in the outside air and heavy dews soaked the grass, Bobbin snuggled up to a hot water bottle as we tried to keep warm in the tent.

Bobbin loved his holidays; but he was always glad to be home, and then for days he would luxuriate in the comfort of his familiar bed, dreaming dreams of triumphs and discoveries which only the three of us had known. Now that he is older, his energies are lower. But I think that if a horsebox pulled up outside our house, he would be ready to go once again ....

Chapter 15: Not So Tough Dog

Dogs are very individual creatures. To understand a dog can be, as any friend of a dog will know, as intricate and absorbing a task as really getting to know another human being. The most significant difference is that a dog is always totally honest; he makes no attempt to conceal his feelings, and he does not harbour grudges. Bobbin, like every other dog and human being, has his own individual personality; and it has been a constant source of enrichment, little by little, to discover his likes and dislikes, to know what delights and what worries him.

I know how he loves to have a pillow to rest his head on. I know how his bed time is half past ten, and how after that time he will seek out the darkest corner of the room, and look disgruntled until I, too, remember that it's time for bed. I know how when he is cold he will go and sit resolutely in front of the fan heater, willing me to switch it on. I know how he can tell me what he wants, simply by the way he looks at me. Learning to understand Bobbin, and to respect him for who he is, has brought me great joy. In return, as I have come to know him better, I have done my best to take account of his preferences, and to do all that I can to let him be himself, and lead as full a life as he can.

Like most terriers, Bobbin has a proud and independent spirit; he is not going to be anybody's fool - or anybody's lap dog either. As he began to grow out of puppyhood, he gradually became more and more scornful of any kind of fuss or display of affection. Of course he always makes sure to position himself so that he can see exactly what everyone else is doing; but he himself prefers to maintain a discreet distance. With human beings he is at times aloof to the point of being needlessly off-hand. If ever he is compelled to sit on someone's knee, he wears an expression of acute disdain: and the moment he senses that his captor is not quite concentrating, he springs free with a look of undisguised relief. Sometimes, if you are very quiet, he might sit down quite close to you - but not too close: if you reach out to pat him, he will be off.

Kindly strangers, charmed by Bobbin's benign and friendly appearance, and enchanted by his large and soulful eyes, frequently have an impulse to bend down and stroke him. These attentions Bobbin dodges as though he had been assaulted: and perhaps he thinks he has. After all, if some total stranger came up to you, told you how nice you are, and without further ado began to pat your posterior or to fondle your ears, how would you feel? When dogs can be represented in parliament, the first thing Bobbin will do will be to introduce a bill to outlaw Dog Harassment and Dog Abuse. Is it surprising, when a dog has to spend all his life with only humans as peers and role models, that at times he acts just like a human being?

Fiercely independent, proud and naturally bold, Bobbin has time and again demonstrated his fearlessness in seeking to defend his loved ones. When he encounters something which fills him, in his turn, with a nameless terror, how miserably helpless I feel that I can do nothing to allay his fears as he has so often allayed mine.

The first problem was fireworks. Not surprisingly, most dogs are terrified of fireworks. The meaningless onset of loud explosions is enough to terrify anyone: how can a dog guess that it is all supposed to be for fun? From the start Bobbin has always become inconsolably hysterical whenever he hears a firework. All his jauntiness disappears in an instant, and he begins to shiver with fear. There is nothing that can calm him. He scorns the comfort of sitting on my knee, and he is too intelligent to imagine that hiding under the sofa could bring any relief. Driven by panic, he seeks escape by racing round and round the room, shaking from head to foot, and with a heart rate approximately four times the normal.

If he is wretched, then I am no less so. It is quite obvious that this state of terror subjects his whole system to an unsustainable strain; and all I can do is to try to take him out of earshot of the distressing noises. More than once, regardless of the time, or any other plans, I have had to set off into the night careless of where we went, if only we could find somewhere safe from the sound of fireworks.

Luckily Bobbin has always had some very good friends. On one memorable night we had just returned from mucking out when still in my grubby jeans I began to wash my hair. Suddenly there was an ear-splitting explosion, followed by the screaming whizz of a rocket, and a long series of spluttering pops. I had completely forgotten that there was to be a firework display that evening following a local fête.

On hearing the first bang, Bobbin had nearly leapt out of his skin. Already he was shaking violently, his eyes horribly glazed and his tongue lolling miserably from his mouth as he rushed panting up and down the stairs and over the furniture. There was no time to finish rinsing my hair; shampoo or not, Bobbin came first.

Quickly flinging an old towel around my head, I grabbed a blanket, and caught the panic-stricken dog. He shook and struggled so fiercely I could hardly keep hold of him, but I threw him into the car and with no clear idea of what to do next, drove off into the darkness.

In our hills and valleys, sounds tend to echo around the whole neighbourhood, and wherever we drove, even with the car radio turned to maximum volume, the sound of the rockets was still reaching Bobbin's terrified ears. It seemed that the only hope of getting him calmed down would be to find some form of distraction .... but where could we go at this time of the evening, and in this unsociable state?

Then I remembered Peter. Peter was a good friend: a gentle, quietly-spoken man, who for twenty years had tended the gardens at the big house near Cookie's field. Raised on a Suffolk farm, he had a natural empathy with all animals, and he often looked after Cookie if I was away. Peter and Doreen loved Bobbin: which was just as well. We arrived at their house, when they were in the middle of a family reunion. With all possible kindness they welcomed us into their home as unexpected guests, apparently failing to be surprised by my dishevelled and distinctly ungroomed appearance. Bobbin lay shivering under their table, but at last, comforted by the seven sets of feet around him, and lulled by the friendly voices inside and the silence outside, he gradually began to calm down.

Naturally I have always made every effort to find out in advance about any firework displays in our area. But around November Fifth, it seems that every night for three weeks before and after, some fun-loving child

For Love of a Dog

somewhere likes to let off the odd banger; and above all the noise that television and radio can make between them, Bobbin invariably hears it and begins to quake. After hearing just one bang, he may well continue in a state of terrified shivering, always listening for the next explosion, for over an hour. There are those who complain that their dogs bark when they hear fireworks - and oh, how lucky they are! There is nothing more painful than to have to watch your best friend suffering in a state of abject terror, and to know that there is almost nothing you can do to help.

Thunderstorms have always been just as alarming, but even more difficult to predict or to avoid. In the summer months I listen avidly to every weather forecast, but there is no way of accurately anticipating exactly when or where the thunder will be. After years of practice, I have become almost as scared of thunder as Bobbin is; but it is harder to drive away from a thunderstorm, and we simply have to sit it out. Even with curtains drawn, Bobbin's eyes will be fixed on one window after another as he pants round the house, desperately searching for a refuge from this incomprehensible threat.

When he was younger, a dose of tranquillizer might help to calm him. Even this was seldom effective, since it was supposed to be administered half an hour before the fright began, which was usually an impossibility. But after a while, he developed a bad reaction to this drug, and other remedies seemed to be of no avail. It is only latterly, as he has grown older, that increasing deafness has begun to bring some relief. Now, if I immediately turn the volume of music as high as possible, there is some chance that he will not hear the sounds that so terrify him. The regular, soothing rhythm of classical music seems to give him a sense of hope and peace.

Gradually his anxiety about thunder and fireworks has led to fears of other alarming noises. Having once been alarmed by the whooshing of a hot air balloon overhead, always since then he has been panic-stricken at the merest glimpse of one, however far away. It is bad enough when he sees one: but he also seems to know when to expect them. If the day is cloudy, or windy, or if it is the middle of winter, Bobbin has no worries. But as soon as there is a day of cloudless blue skies in the spring or summer, his walks are beset by anxiety. He keeps glancing anxiously up at the sky, as if he knows that this is exactly the sort of day when a hot air balloon might suddenly appear.

At times he has shown what appears to be almost a sixth sense about this particular danger. On more than one occasion, we have been travelling over the Hog's Back, high above the surrounding Surrey landscape, when far away to the south I have spotted a hot air balloon. Bobbin is sleeping peacefully on the seat beside me. "It's all right," I think. "That must be fifteen miles away: he can't possibly hear it." Then, as if he were reading my thoughts, he suddenly sits bolt upright, looks straight at the speck in the sky as though I had pointed to it, and tries to dive for cover. I have no idea how he knows. But infallibly he does.

Certainly Bobbin has incredibly good eyesight. He can follow the path of an overflying aircraft even when it is barely larger than a pinprick in the distance: fortunately, the sound of aircraft engines or helicopters does not alarm him. He watches with interest as microlights glide silently overhead: but kites are another matter. The first time he saw a kite was when we were on Weymouth beach, and he was instantly terrified. He tried so hard to bolt in his panic that, as on many another occasion, to prevent him choking himself on his collar, the only solution was to pick him up and try to ignore his scrabbling claws as we hastened back to the car. Many a time since then a relaxing walk to a well-loved viewpoint has ended in disorganised retreat when we have come upon some happy children innocently trying to fly a kite.

For Love of a Dog

Bobbin's anxieties appear to be triggered by things which make a sound that he interprets as a signal of danger: fireworks, thunder, hot air balloons, flapping kites: and finally rain. His fear of the sound of rain began quite suddenly, and nearly had disastrous results. We were coming home from Dorset one evening when we drove into a cloudburst. Bobbin, lying beside me on the passenger seat, looked a little fidgety, but I could see no cause for alarm. Then, suddenly, an oncoming lorry launched a torrent of spray over our windscreen. It did make an alarming splash, but nothing could have prepared me for Bobbin's reaction. In a split second he was in panic mode. He leapt on to my knee, on to my shoulder, off again, and began hurtling all round the car. We were in a steady stream of traffic, on a main road, and could not stop immediately. Before we had reached a spot where we could safely pull over, Bobbin had dived into the floor well and lodged himself resolutely between my feet and the control pedals.

Coping with a panic-stricken dog is never an easy matter. But the situation was now really dangerous. I couldn't brake, I couldn't change gear. With a supreme effort, I at last managed to wrench him out, and hurl him on to the back seat. He was determined to return to this refuge which he evidently regarded as the safest place, and I can remember, as I battled to keep control of the steering, consciously trying to stun him in an effort to subdue his struggles. Whatever I did to him now would be preferable to a head on collision. I turned up the very first track we came to, and I remember Bobbin trying to bolt from the car towards the misty hills.

After administering a double dose of tranquillizers and waiting forty minutes for them to take effect, we were at last able to leave that desolate spot. For the remainder of the journey, Bobbin sat on my knee, shaking convulsively, but at least unable now to charge around the car. It had been a very near thing. For a long time we did not attempt any car journey when there was heavy rain; and nowadays he is always safely strapped into a dog harness.

My inability to comfort Bobbin when he is overcome by irrational fears is a failure which it is hard to accept. I wish so much that I could protect him from his fears just as he has so often protected me. There is nothing more saddening than to witness the sudden transformation of my normally confident, bright-eyed, independent friend into a shaking bundle of inconsolable terror, and I would do anything in the world to help him to meet these unseen dangers with his usual debonair courage. But try as I may, I simply have not found a way.

Chapter 16: Visits To The Vet

Almost as bad as thunder and fireworks are visits to the vet; and over the years there have been all too many of these.

Although we have never yet met a vet who was anything other than gentle and caring, I have come to dread these encounters almost as much as Bobbin does. As soon as we approach the surgery, all his heroic Jack Russell spirit seems to evaporate. His eyes cloud over, his tail is wedged firmly between his legs, and he begins to shiver uncontrollably. Yet once again, to my chagrin, there is almost nothing I can do to reassure him - except for taking him straight out of the door again.

Bobbin seems to have an instinct about vets which it is hard to understand. One Sunday evening when he was unwell, we had to attend a veterinary surgery we had not visited before. As we drove along, he was lying quietly in the car, apparently unsuspecting; but as soon as we pulled up across the road from the surgery, he sat up with a bleak look that wrenched my heart with its expression of betrayal and foreboding. Drooping his ears disconsolately, he began to shake, and his eyes held a look of abject misery. How he knew, I cannot guess. But he knows. Even if I speak to his vet on the telephone, he knows: and he at once wakes up and regards me with an unhappy look of reproach, as if he understands exactly what I am planning.

Bobbin spurns to be a lap dog; in his view, physical contact with human beings is best kept to a minimum. The only exception is when he is really in need of security. Then, and only then, he seems to gain some comfort from sitting on my shoulder. When he was a puppy, he used to enjoy lying behind my neck; but he has long since grown out of this cosy habit. Yet when he feels that special danger is threatening - the danger of a visit to the vet - and lateral escape is impossible, he still adopts the vertical method.

Perhaps he hopes that if he stays very close, the vet will end up examining me by mistake. At the very least, he ensures that I have no choice but to suffer with him.

I do not mind at all having Bobbin sitting on my shoulder. If he hangs on with his front feet, and looks out over my back, his tail provides a useful handle; and in this position he stays sufficiently still for the vet to examine him. Sometimes, as a variation, he likes to lie across my back, with his feet forward over my shoulders, and this is quite comfortable too. He has even managed on many occasions to clamber up to this perch, just for the fun of it, when we are riding; and provided that we are not trying to get somewhere at great speed, it can be a perfectly satisfactory arrangement.

But what is less appealing is the suddenness and vigour of his ascent; my flesh being quite soft, he is able to find very good footholds by digging in his claws. The advantage of this method is that Bobbin is in little danger of slipping, but the disadvantage is that I find it rather painful. Still, you can't have everything: a few drops of blood is not a very high price to pay if it helps to change a nervous and miserable dog into a slightly more contented and secure one.

It is hard to know why it is that Bobbin seems to have had more than his fair share of troubles over the years. Perhaps some weakness was triggered by his bad response to his vaccination in puppyhood. But when I hear my friends complaining about the high cost of the yearly boosters, I listen with envy - if only that were all!

Some problems have persistently plagued Bobbin since he was quite small. The most recurrent is his tender digestive system, which suffers from all kinds of maladies. I have met people who, in blissful ignorance, seem to think that a dog's digestion is as tough as old boots. If there are any who enjoy this fortunate state of affairs, Bobbin is not one of them. Sometimes he can scarcely be induced to eat at all; sometimes he has a ravenous appetite for no apparent reason. There are times when he is sick after every meal, and times when he suffers with grumbling abdominal pains. No matter how careful I am about how much food I give him and when, his sickness recurs time and again. I have lost count of how many times the vet has been consulted, and of the different diagnoses, which have included colic, colitis, hiatus hernia, and duodenal ulcer. Sometimes the treatments work, sometimes they don't. I would give a very great deal to any vet who could really find the cure.

As if it was not enough to be plagued by a difficult digestive system, another source of suffering has always been his very pink and sensitive skin. Animals with dark skins are far more resistant to the kind of troubles that Bobbin has had to endure. Over the years, I have racked my brains to try to pin-point a pattern of cause and effect, but always this has been inconclusive. His suffering has been attributed variously and vaguely to different types of dermatitis or unidentifiable allergies. Dust mites or harvest mites surely take their toll, but without doubt the flea is his worst enemy. A single bite from a flea can inflame his skin for days.

This itching is no joke; night after night we are both kept awake by Bobbin's frantic efforts to bite and chew the pain away, and by the inevitable choking on the mouthfuls of hair which he ingests in the process. Summer is the worst time, and we have to be assiduously careful about which friends we visit.

"Oh, Susie doesn't have fleas!" our friend says airily, "I never see her scratching!" But that evening, without fail, Bobbin becomes demented, biting at his itch until his skin is red and raw. And sure enough, I usually find a beastly little black stow-away wandering through what's left of his fur. It's just that Susie is lucky enough not to be allergic to flea bites.

There are flea treatments in plenty that will kill the flea: but not until it has had its one disastrous bite. In earlier days, cortisone was effective in relieving his distress; but now that Bobbin is older, that, too, has undesirable side-effects. We have tried countless antihistamines, diet supplements, baths, and homeopathic remedies .... and we still live in hope.

But Bobbin is a very good patient. Reluctant but cooperative, when his feet are itchy, he submits to having little socks tied on to his paws, so that he can't chew himself lame; and he is almost enthusiastic about being given pills. None of those problems of disguising the remedy in a tempting parcel of butter or tasty meat with Bobbin: just mention the word pill, and he trots over and sits down looking up expectantly, as though this attention were a special privilege. But attempting to apply soothing creams or lotions is another matter entirely. This comes under the heading of unwarranted interference, and is vigorously resisted with scrabbling claws and wounded looks of angry outrage.

For Love of a Dog

Between these bouts of regular troubles, there have been many other alarms. There was the time when he accidentally swallowed some yew leaves, and had to be rushed to the vet and be induced to vomit. There was the time when he unaccountably picked up kennel cough although he had not been anywhere with other dogs for several days; and there have been throat infections, ear infections, and tooth infections. There was the time when he developed an abscess on his tummy which burst while he was secreted in my five-star hotel room at a management conference. And once, after a long hot car journey in summer, in spite of frequent stops by cool shady streams, his heart was unable to cope with the heat, and he had to have diuretics to clear the fluid from his lungs. The diuretics affected his kidneys, and he was unwell for weeks.

Slowly, I have learnt how to avoid some of these dangers. I take care that he doesn't lick his paws if he has been near any yew trees, and if we really cannot avoid travelling on a hot day, Bobbin always travels wrapped in a damp towel, with a battery-operated fan ready as backup nearby. Prevention is better than cure, but some things take a lot of preventing: it is so easy to be wise after the event.

There was the time - the only time that Bobbin's charisma was ineffective - when a Doberman bitch made a completely unprovoked attack on him in a stable yard and savagely ripped a piece out of his shoulder. Bobbin's cries were terrible to hear. It was just as well that she got hold of him near the water tank so that it was possible to break up the fight before any more damage was done. Not that it was a fight, exactly. I don't think Bobbin so much as laid a paw on her in self-defence. The pain and shock of her unexpected attack plunged him into a state of panic. As soon as she let go of him, he raced round and round the yard in a demented frenzy, and it was some time before we could corner him in a stable and catch him up in a towel to rush him off to the vet for a neat bit of emergency stitching.

One of his most lucky escapes, however, was the time he was stung by a wasp. For some inexplicable reason, Bobbin has always been terrified by the sight or sound of a fly. Often in the evening when we are sitting peacefully at home, suddenly Bobbin leaps up with an expression of dejected misery and is desperate to go outside. Once the door is opened, he seizes the chance of escape. Out he goes into the garden and sits down, with an unhappy and watchful look, facing the back door, as though he feels he is at a safe distance now. By searching carefully, I can usually track down the origin of this behaviour to the presence of a bluebottle or housefly in the room. Unless it can be banished, Bobbin refuses to come back in. There then follow ten or fifteen minutes of strategic turning off and on of lights and opening and shutting of doors. First I turn off all the sitting room lights, and leave the lobby light on: then watch and wait. When it seems that the offending insect has entered the lobby, the study lights are turned on, and the lobby lights off. If the fly once again obligingly follows the light, then I shut it in the study and try to remember not to let it out accidentally. If we are upstairs, it has to be manoeuvred into a spare bedroom and let out of the window in the morning.

Yet unaccountably - and this is the one thing in which Bobbin fails to show his usual good sense - he has never had any fear of wasps. Instead of steering clear of wasps and bees, he does the worst thing possible and tries to catch them. This means that he can never be left unsupervised in the garden in late summer, and it is not a good idea to leave him in a car with the windows open. In spite of these assiduous precautions, one day the inevitable happened.

It was a warm July day, and we were expecting visitors for lunch. Being preoccupied with the preparations, I neglected to supervise Bobbin who was sitting on the front door step in doleful anticipation. Just as Mary and Ros arrived, Bobbin ran in, looking a little agitated, and for a moment I wondered if he was all right.

"He looks all right to me!" they said cheerfully, and on we went with the lunch.

From time to time during the afternoon he looked rather out of sorts, but there did not seem to be anything obviously wrong. It was not until eight o'clock that evening that I knew for certain that all was not well. Bobbin was repeatedly trying to eat grass to make himself sick - not just a bit of grass, but handfuls of grass: pounds of grass, and no kind of dissuasion could make him stop. By nine o'clock I was seriously worried and made an appointment for an immediate visit to the vet. By this time he was convulsively retching and coughing, and still desperately swallowing quantities of grass whenever he got the chance.

"I'll give him something to calm him down. He should go to sleep.... But don't let him eat any more grass."

Sleep! That night there was no such possibility. No longer allowed access to grass, Bobbin now began to eat the carpet. In between snatching mouthfuls as though his life depended on it, which in a way it did, Bobbin was now racing up and down panting and coughing continuously. By midnight we were back at the vet's. But still he had no idea what was causing the trouble. I think the vet thought I was a rather neurotic owner - he may well have been right - but that was certainly not the root of the problem. He gave him something stronger to "settle him down" and home we went, hoping against hope that now the frenzy might begin to abate.

The hours between midnight and four in the morning were some of the least pleasant I can remember. They were spent on the bathroom floor, with Bobbin shackled to me by his lead. Even here he was trying desperately to eat the pattern off the linoleum, while I struggled to keep him from exhausting himself even more by his attempts to rush up and down, apparently in a hopeless effort to escape his discomfort. But nothing I could do was of any avail. By four o'clock, Bobbin appeared to be on the point of collapse, and we got the poor vet out of bed yet again. I think he was at his wits' end, too, and he said that nothing more could be done till morning - unless I would like him to admit him, and leave him in a cage at the back of the surgery for the rest of the night. How could I leave Bobbin on his own when he was clearly in such distress? Instead, I resorted to driving him round in the car until daybreak, when he eventually fell asleep; and, parked in a car park somewhere in Surrey, I fell into an exhausted half-sleep on top of him.

The next day he was admitted as an in-patient. Blood tests were taken: they showed that he had an infected sting. As this was presumably in his throat, he had literally been fighting for his life all night long, and at last we understood why he had felt compelled to swallow anything he could, and to cough: it had been a futile attempt to clear the painful blockage from his throat. The following night we both slept very well.

For Love of a Dog

In spite of his horror of visiting the vet, and the increasing frequency of his visits, Bobbin has always been a long-suffering and well-mannered patient. He forgives his tormentor time and again for his unsolicited pawing and probing. But there was one occasion when the poor practitioner got more than he had bargained for. Bobbin had been shaking his head as if he had some discomfort, and it seemed best to have his ears checked. The vet on duty happened to be a new vet, a locum from New Zealand; and Mr. Bridger was obviously rather nervous of Jack Russells.
"You never know with terriers," he said, "They can be a bit unpredictable. I think I'd better sedate him first."

This seemed a little unnecessary, but I agreed: after all, the vet knows best. Having established that Bobbin's ears were, as he put it, "cleaner than if I had syringed them myself", he suggested checking his teeth while he was *hors de combat*.

Gently he began to prise open Bobbin's mouth: and then suddenly there was a terrible snap. Bobbin's jaws clamped shut. His canine teeth had pierced right through Mr. Bridger's index finger.
"I'd forgotten," he said, as the colour drained from his tanned cheeks, "That their jaw has an automatic reflex action when they are unconscious."
Fortunately, the next client in the waiting room was a springer spaniel, accompanied by his owner, the local doctor.

Sometimes it seems that Bobbin has had more than his share of troubles. A dog, just like the rest of us, has to take the rough with the smooth. But when you see him racing across a grassy field, as if he hadn't a care in the world, it's hard to remember that he ever had a pain.

Chapter 17: Understanding Each Other

If I have grown over the years to understand Bobbin, his joys and his troubles, then he has just as surely learned to understand me. For over fourteen years he has been watching, studying, interpreting and remembering everything that his human companions say, do - and even think. He has stored in his brain a vast range of clues which tell him what is going to happen, and what it means for him and his friends. Some of these clues are transparently obvious, many are less easy for us humans of little brain to understand.

I have learnt to understand how Bobbin is feeling from how he is lying: whether he lies curled and tight (he is cold, or miserable); stretched on his side (he is tired and wants to sleep); or upside down with his paws in the air (he is completely relaxed and happy). I have learnt from the angle of his jaw, and the set of his mouth, to recognise when he has a pain. I know when he looks at me whether he is asking for food, or a walk; and whether he is really hungry or just bored. I know which dogs he enjoys meeting, and which of our friends he most likes to visit. I know which paths he prefers to walk on, and I know when he is out of sorts and does not feel like walking at all. I know that he hates the smell of perfume because it makes him sneeze, and I know how he sits hunched up, with his back turned, when he feels left out or disappointed. I know when he has a sparkle in his eye that today he is feeling really good, and would like to do something special.

All of this is very basic; it does not amount to enough for an O Level, let alone a PhD. It is as nothing to the vast and accurate store of knowledge that Bobbin has amassed about my world: the world of humans, which has been, for all of his life, such a large part of his world, too.

Of course, like any reasonably intelligent dog, he has learnt to a very nice degree about those aspects of housekeeping which have particular relevance to his main interests. He can quickly identify a refrigerator in anyone's kitchen; he can spot the cupboard with the biscuits in, and he knows where to ask for a drink of water. He could, until quite recently, hear from a surprising distance when anyone opened the door of a fridge: and no matter where he had been, or how sound asleep, he would be there in a matter of seconds - politely suggesting that you might like to look and see if there is any ham in there ....

With Bobbin in the house, it is not possible to have a bite of a biscuit, let alone a chocolate, unless I am planning to share it. He always knows. He knows, too, when I am cooking some fresh chicken for him. Every other day a fresh casserole of chicken and brown rice goes into the oven just for him; and it is so much tastier when it is straight from the oven. Yesterday's is just not good enough. Rather than make do with second best, Bobbin will wait politely between his plate and the cooker, emphasising his patience with an occasional pathetic shiver. I have to be very careful about the timing when I cook his chicken, or yesterday's will be wasted.

For years Bobbin has refused to condescend to consume any kind of tinned or processed food - with one unexpected exception. He has of late developed a decided partiality for a particular brand of cat food which one of our neighbours frequently feeds to her cats. Whenever we pass her house, he keeps a close look out. He has worked out that if the children are playing in the garden, then the back door is likely to be open - and he is gone like a flash. It is lucky for him that he has such a charismatic knack of winning friends.

The hardest thing a dog has to understand is where he fits in to our human social life. The way that humans behave towards each other must be quite difficult enough for a plain-thinking, honest dog to follow; but to grasp the role that he is expected to play must be even harder. Sometimes he is treated as an equal member of the pack, and sometimes he is not. He may expect to be welcomed warmly when we go visiting, but he must not expect that he may share the delectable chocolate cake he can smell; if he gets anything it will probably be a dry biscuit. Others may lounge on the sofa, but he must stay on the drafty floor. Others may help themselves to the bar of chocolate, but if he even licks it, he is in disgrace. It is hardly surprising that even the best-intentioned dog may sometimes make a mistake.

In his younger days, Bobbin was always delighted when friends came to visit us, and he joined in the camaraderie with energy and enthusiasm. He would try his very best to take part, making it clear that he expected to be accepted as an equal (or more than equal) member of the group. Grabbing hold of anything - cushion, shoe, or soft toy - that came to hand, or tooth, he would toss it wildly around, making sure that he got his share of attention. He was expressing his delight in the only way he could. He was not able to join in the niceties of our polite conversation, but in his own special way he contributed his very best offerings of goodwill.

As he has grown older, Bobbin has become slightly less tolerant - or is it more discerning? - about the presence of visitors. If he has been forewarned, he is usually pleased to greet people when they arrive. But perhaps, as his skill in understanding the verbal system of human communication has grown, he has begun to feel more confused or hurt if he feels he is being heedlessly left out. Our stimulating conversation runs on and on, and he seems to have no part to play in it. He does his best to be polite for a while, but there are limits; and nowadays he harbours very definite ideas about how long a guest should stay. Perhaps he also objects to having his routine interrupted, and to the disturbance to his increasing need for sleep.

Whatever his reasons, he has developed an effective personal system of communicating his point of view. When he begins to feel that a guest has stayed long enough - and I have to admit that there have been times when I myself have been stifling a yawn - he first of all begins to glare at me in a peculiar and uncompromising way. When there is no response to this, he expresses his resentment by an impressively articulate range of vocalisations. At first, accompanied by a little shiver, he makes a low and plaintive sound, very softly, like a tentative arpeggio on the cello. If this elicits no response, he begins, quietly at first, to run up and down the scale. As the minutes tick by, Bobbin's utterances become gradually more *vibrato* and urgent. He varies the melody, and increases the scope of tone and pitch: he alternates between tremolos and *glissandi*; at one moment he quavers *sotto voce* like the trill of a bassoon, at another he seems to be warming up for the soprano role in *La Sonnambula*.

I wish I had a good enough command of his language to be able to describe the wide range of sounds which Bobbin utters. Certainly they are neither growl, nor bark, nor whine. It seems that he is using all that he has learnt over the years of listening to human speech to do his utmost to find words to join in the conversation, or to add his protests when he feels he is not being properly included. It is a source of enduring regret to me, and frustration to him, that the human range of consonants and vowels is beyond the capabilities of his vocal chords. But the intonations aren't. Sadness, reproach, resentment, frustration, sometimes even anger - the tones, and the pitch, of his utterances are unmistakable, and compelling.

Silently, I listen with fascination, and I long to congratulate Bobbin on the range and talent of his repertoire. But aloud, in the interests of decorum, I am obliged to exclaim, "Oh dear, Bobbin! Whatever is the matter?" and apologetically add to our guest, "I really can't think what it is." But whatever excuses I come up with, I think his meaning is usually all too clear to our friend, too. At any rate, as our ability to concentrate on the conversation becomes increasingly impeded by the punctuation of

Bobbin's insistent crescendo of pleas, he usually achieves his goal. Our guest suddenly realises how late it is.

It would scarcely be fair to rebuke Bobbin for his contributions. They are his response to the social pressures to which, through no choice of his own, he is subjected. He makes such a strenuous effort to communicate with us, just as he hears us communicating with each other, that the least we can do is to give him credit for his achievements, and do our best to listen to what he has to say. After all, our monotonous verbalisations probably sound as meaningless to him as his do to the humans who wish to restrict their interactivity to their own species.

Like most dogs, Bobbin appears to have a sixth sense about strangers. If a workman comes to fix a tap, or paint a door, once he has been introduced Bobbin quickly accepts the newcomer and generally shows no further interest. This person is not going to waste our time and take up my attention with useless chat; he is not worth bothering with. Only once did he take a different attitude. I needed a window fixing, and a neighbour had an odd job man working on her garage. We arranged that before he went home, he would come and repair our window.

Doug seemed a pleasant enough chap: but as soon as he came into the house, his eyes were everywhere. Unlike most workmen, he began to scan the ornaments and pictures with keen interest, and began asking all sorts of questions about them. I suppose it made me feel a little uncomfortable: it would have been much better if he had concentrated on the job in hand. But Bobbin took an instant and resolute dislike to him. He could hardly be persuaded to desist from the most menacing growls and barks, and never for one moment did he take his eyes off the workman until he had mended the hinges and shaken our dust from off his feet. I felt relieved too; I had an uncanny feeling that Bobbin knew something that I didn't.

Bobbin's own special insight has been informative in many ways and on many occasions. More than once, he has been less than enthusiastic about a colleague or acquaintance whom I later discovered was not as trustworthy as I had thought; and I have learnt to respect and trust his judgement as being often more perceptive than my own.

In recent years, Bobbin no longer needed to be left at home while I was working, but came with me and spent his days sleeping soundly under my desk. He quickly understood the routine: colleagues and visitors were constantly coming and going all day long, and he took no notice of them at all. This was his chance for a good sleep; he knew that during working hours he must keep out of the way, and leave me to get on with my work uninterrupted. But if I was alone in the building, working late after everyone else had gone home, then it was a different matter; then, if any strange car drew up outside, or if he heard someone come to the door he would bark just as if he were at home.

My office was upstairs, and if no one was about downstairs it was perfectly possible for someone to enter the front door unnoticed. One morning, Bobbin had been soundly asleep and sweetly dreaming, when he suddenly leapt up and began barking ferociously. I had heard nothing; but it was so unusual for him to bark that I went down straight away to investigate - and there was a most disreputable-looking tramp. Once again I had reason to be grateful to Bobbin. Somehow, his instincts had told him that on this occasion he must break the unspoken rules: I needed to know who had come into the building.

But Bobbin's most complete understanding of the world around him comes from his ability to understand me, and to know what I am going to do before I tell him. With uncanny astuteness, he has learned to read dozens of tiny signs and signals of which I am often not conscious. Day after day, year after year he has quietly watched me, and now he knows better than I do what I usually do when, and what I shall probably do next.

To my way of thinking, there are more important things in life than being house-proud; which is just as well, since everything in our house is interwoven with a fine and ineradicable surplus of tough white hairs, the product of Bobbin's perpetual moult. But if a visitor is expected, I generally run the hoover over the floor as best I can. This in itself is not enough to tell Bobbin that someone is about to arrive: occasionally the floor is vacuumed for no reason other than that it seems time. But there must be other tiny signals: for if someone is about to arrive for a visit, Bobbin unfailingly knows. He will not settle; instead, he sits waiting by the door, or if possible by the gate, ready to greet our guest. He is quick to hear the sound of the strange car engine, even though visitors to our house have to park a little way down the lane. When at last our guests arrive, he rushes up and down in excitement, letting them know that they are expected, and that they are welcome: that he is prepared.

It is always better to tell Bobbin in advance exactly who is coming, or where we are going. He is always happier when he knows he has been included in any plans. But if for some reason he is not given adequate warning - if, for example, a friend calls unexpectedly - he makes it very clear that he thinks it most discourteous that he was not consulted; and he screws up the mat or launches at once into one of his favourite arias. Sometimes he is mollified if I explain that they won't be staying long ....

It is not easy to fool Bobbin. There are no prizes for knowing when we are going on holiday: the sight of a luggage bag is an obvious give-away. But he knows my habits so well that he can always tell for certain even if I am only thinking about going to the shops. Time and again I have tried to work out what are the clues that tell him I am about to go out.

Obviously, if I were to get a bag, or a coat, my intentions would be quite clear. But he knows far ahead of that.

During the day, if I am at home, in the course of things I naturally have to go upstairs, or into the bathroom, several times on different errands. Bobbin sleeps soundly on. But when I go into the bathroom and start to put on perfume or lipstick, within seconds there is an anxious black and white face with tentatively questioning eyes peeping round the door. I can understand the perfume - with his nose he could smell that from anywhere - but *lipstick?* He seems to know even when I am thinking of combing my hair.

Of course the most telling signals are given through the clothes that I put on. Bobbin has spent years studying my clothes, and each morning, he watches carefully to see what type of apparel I select. Everyone wears different clothes for different occasions, and Bobbin has become a canine expert in couture. He knows as well as anyone exactly what kinds of clothes are worn for different types of activity. You can't have much fun in a skirt: and the smarter the skirt the less fun it is likely to be. For years Bobbin had to endure, as I did, the necessity of looking smart for work, and smarter still for special meetings. He accepted without protest that this was going to be a dull day. But a skirt on a non-working day was a cause for real alarm. Was he going to be able to come? What was I going to do? Had I, by some terrible chance, forgotten about him? His anxious eyes would focus in forlorn concentration on my every move, until he could no longer endure the uncertainty; and then he would run backwards and forwards, making mute appeals to me not to forget him, and jumping up and down on the spot with excitement as if to remind me that he was game for anything and would be no trouble at all, if only I would take him with me.

Then again, there is always the chance that I might start off the day in casual clothes, but change later on. If I go upstairs to fetch a book, he is not bothered. But if I go upstairs and start to change my clothes (and I don't think I make very much noise about it) then straight away little feet come leaping up the stairs and an accusing expression challenges me to explain what I am planning. With alert and anxious eyes he watches closely as I go to the wardrobe, and studies the portentous garments with profound concern.

Even now, when all our days are non-working days, there are still occasional moments of apprehension. The appearance of something different - a new pair of trousers, or an unaccustomed pair of shoes - provokes particular consternation. No other friend is so observant about what I am wearing, or so quick to notice when something is new. With the greatest attention, Bobbin sniffs the unfamiliar garment up and down, pausing occasionally as if there were some particular piece of the fabric which concealed a vital clue. Whatever he discovers is well beyond my powers of comprehension.

Although Bobbin accepted the necessity of going to work in boring clothes, and having only a fraction of the day left for getting on with real life, there were times when he would do his best to ensure that his point of view could not be completely ignored, particularly if he sensed that today was somehow different - most notably if I was attending an especially important conference.

Fortunately there were few days when it was not possible for me to take Bobbin with me in the car. He has always loved staying in the car, and once left he settles into a contented and blissful sleep. Even if it were an all-day meeting, there would still be coffee and lunch breaks when I could take him for a breath of fresh air, instead of devouring Danish pastries with my colleagues.

But on these days Bobbin made sure that while I was away from him, his presence would still be felt. Actions, as every dog knows, so often speak louder than words. When he saw that I had put on a smarter than usual new black suit, he would swallow all his pride in order to make his point. Then, and only then, he would insist on sitting on my knee for just long enough to ensure that I arrived amply coated in those familiar white hairs which meant that even in his absence my friend could not be forgotten.

For several miles I would resist his attempts with vigour; but at last, I would say to myself, " After all, what is more important? Trying to look smart in the eyes of a few colleagues - or the happiness of my dearest friend?" Of course, there was no real contest.

But the best days have always been the days when there was no going to work, and Bobbin would watch with scarcely containable delight as I reached for my old jeans and T-shirt. Now he knew that today was going to be a day for him, and he would race up and down with impatience to be off. I am glad, for his sake, that nowadays these days are the norm: his years of quiet waiting are behind him.

It is hard not to be impressed by the extent of Bobbin's skills and accuracy in interpreting the human world around him. Many of his instincts I cannot even begin to understand. But of one thing I have become ever more certain. The extent of Bobbin's knowledge about life, about his human companion, and about many of those other people he has come into contact with, is certainly not inferior to my own. Unlike my view of the world, his is not cluttered with preconceptions, or limited by attempts at rationality and the habits of politeness. His reliance on instinct has not been tempered by the conventions of civilisation. His judgement is based on his own observations and perceptions; it is candid and unaffected; it is often more unerring than my own. And there have been many occasions when I should have given a lot to be able to know what it is that he knows, and to see as clearly as he can see.

Chapter 18: These Humans !

With the aid of his highly-developed senses, Bobbin is able to make sense of what he sees, what he hears, and what he can smell. But equally keen, and less easy to account for, is his remarkable instinct for picking up moods: not only my moods, but also other people's. In many ways Bobbin's behaviour can be taken as an indicator - like a sort of litmus test - of the atmosphere among a group of people.

If those around him are happy and bright, Bobbin, too, is bright-eyed, enthusiastic and alert. When he knows that all around him is well, and nothing disturbing is likely to happen, then he can go contentedly to his bed for a sleep. But if there is any tension in the room, he cannot relax, and the degree of malaise is reflected in the agitation of his demeanour.

Some time ago, neighbour of ours was heading for a very unpleasant divorce. Everything her husband did - or didn't do - infuriated her, and she used to come round regularly in order to vent her anger about his latest exploit. Every time she raised her voice, Bobbin shuddered; and after a while, even she noticed that Bobbin was cowering in a corner and shaking. "Oh dear," she said perceptively, "Nigel makes me so angry that even poor Bobbin is upset!" After a while Bobbin was getting so distressed by the sight of Sophie that I had to pretend to be out when she knocked on the door.

Bobbin is a peace-maker. He would like everybody to be friends. Once more, it seems to be he who has more wisdom and magnanimity than often we humans can demonstrate.

But of course it is, unfortunately, my ups and downs that he has to live with: and at times this can be quite a heavy responsibility. It is bad enough feeling depressed, without having to get even more depressed at the thought that you are depressing the dog, who will then chew his paws and make them sore and end with another visit to the vet which will, in turn, make both of us even more depressed.

For Love of a Dog

During one hot August, Bobbin's allergic reaction was yet again triggered by a flea bite. For two days and nights he was ceaselessly tormented by intolerable itching. Nothing seemed to help. His skin was raw and bleeding, and he kept choking on the fur he was swallowing. For two days and nights I had done my best to keep calm and cheerful, and to distract him from his torment. I felt I could do no more. Finally, when we were both at our wits' end with anxiety and exhaustion, I took him as an emergency to the duty vet whom we had not met before.

As Bobbin rushed up and down the surgery in a state of complete hysteria, I collapsed on a windowsill with my head in my hands and started to fret about his panic attack. For a few minutes Miss Page observed us with a coolly professional eye: it did not take her long to sum up the situation. As I attempted in vain to reassure Bobbin, very politely but firmly she said to me, "Will you be quiet? You are making him worse by reinforcing his anxiety. Just leave him alone."

I knew she was right. Bobbin's distress had made me so fraught, that on top of his original malady, he was now also absorbing my acute state of tension. Each of us was becoming more and more anxious, and so neither of us was able to work towards any relief. We had become a vicious circle. "Dogs feel more comfortable when they are around people who breathe deeply," she added meaningly.

I recognised this truth at once - not that it is always very easy to achieve. Bobbin's ideal is for everyone around him to be completely relaxed so that he can relax, too. In the evenings, when he wants to settle down to sleep, and I am still trying to catch up with a few more tasks before I can sit down and rest, Bobbin longs for me to stop what I am doing. At these times, he refuses to go on his bed, but sits and watches me with an expression of profound and reproachful sadness. I know that he will only properly settle down to sleep when I am still, too. What does it matter if the washing-up, or the typing, or the telephone calls are left till tomorrow? It is far better to go and sit down on the sofa for a few minutes. Then, and only then, will he jump up on to his sheepskin and stretch out for a rest.... and (as he probably well knows) I feel much better, too, for having being forced to relax.

I know, too, from countless different occasions when we are visiting friends how carefully Bobbin always selects where to sit when he is in a strange room. When he first enters the room, he pauses for a moment in the doorway, and looks thoughtfully round to see who is there. Then, with an air of decision, he will choose to go and sit beside whoever is most quiet. If they happen to be ensconced in a comfortable arm chair, with a good book, or even better if they are having a doze, he will walk deliberately across the room and curl up at their feet. If, on the other hand, everyone is talking, he sits disconsolately in the middle of the room where he cannot be ignored, and makes plangent contributions to the general conversation.

Now that he is older, even when we are out for a walk, if he comes across someone resting on a wayside seat to admire the view, his expression changes as though he had found a soul-mate, and he trots up and sits quietly down beside them. With that instinct which is more often associated with cats, he unerringly selects those people who are not immediately going to say, "Hello, little fellow!" and try to pat him. I don't know how he knows, but he always gets it right. Perhaps it is something to do with their breathing....

Bobbin's susceptibility to the state of mind of those around him was on one occasion demonstrated beyond all doubt. I had arranged to visit a hypnotherapist near Salisbury. We hadn't been there before and had no idea, until we arrived, that Gaby's sixteenth-century thatched cottage was situated right on the edge of the army firing ranges of Salisbury Plain. From the moment we drew up outside her house, Bobbin lapsed into a state of complete terror. In vain we tried to calm his trembling, or to block out the sound of the explosions. We had come a long way, and I was reluctant to abandon my appointment; and so, with considerable misgivings, we decided to go ahead and hope for the best.

I lay down on the sofa, and to my surprise Bobbin promptly lay down on top of me. He was panting fast and shaking uncontrollably. Gaby put on some suitable music, and quietly began to lead me to breathe deeply and relax. Gradually, in spite of the vibrations from Bobbin's trembling, I slipped into a state of deep, semi-conscious relaxation; and as I did so, I could feel Bobbin's heartbeats slowing down, until he, too, stopped shaking and began to breathe deeply and to fall asleep. Above the sound of his quiet breathing, and Gaby's voice, I could hear that the gunfire was still as loud as before.

It is not surprising that Bobbin has this ability to pick up and respond to moods: awareness of the state of mind of other pack members is essential to the survival of any species, even humans. To the receptive observer, unspoken signals can convey emotions such as fear, anxiety or anger more clearly than all the words with which we try to communicate - or disguise - our true feelings. But this innate sensitivity can be quite unnerving. It means that Bobbin can pick up, and respond to, my moods often before I am aware of them myself.

Although I do not watch very much television, there used to be times when, late at night, exhausted by work, I would switch on the set, content to watch anything as long as it would take my mind off budget forecasts and staffing problems. As this was invariably well after the nine o'clock watershed, I would frequently find that I was glued to some unpleasant murder mystery, or unwholesome drama full of tension and creepy music. Too tired to move, and gripped against my better judgement by an overwhelming desire to see what gruesome thing would happen next, I was unable to summon the strength of will to go to bed. How many times, when later on I was kept awake by visions of aliens swooping down and hiding behind the door, have I wished that I had turned it off sooner!

Bobbin, however, has a great deal more sense than I have. He hates this sort of television. Whether it is the music, or whether he senses my subconscious reaction to the mounting tension, I cannot say. But if I persist in keeping the programme on when the viewing is becoming sinister or violent, it is only in the face of poignant protests from Bobbin. Instead of sleeping quietly beside me, he sits up and stares at me, and begins to shiver, with an expression of deep reproach in his eyes. Many's the time that I have had to apologise to him, and promise not to watch such a programme again.

Bobbin used to love coming to work with me. However busy we were, he would sleep all day, undisturbed by any crises, content to go for a little walk in the field at lunch time, and then drop off to sleep again until it was time to go home. A few years ago, that suddenly changed. It was not until several months later, when I was obliged to take time off work with exhaustion, that I realised that my heavy work load had been taking its toll on my health. I knew that I was working till ridiculously late at night, and starting early in the morning. I knew that living on cereal and occasional cheese sandwiches was not generally speaking regarded as the most energising and balanced diet, but it seemed all right at the time. There were always so many urgent things to do that getting a meal seemed hardly a priority.

But Bobbin knew that something was wrong. Unaccountably, as it seemed to everyone at the time, he began to be fidgety all through the day. Instead of settling down peacefully on his sheepskin under my desk, he would pace restlessly up and down, and wherever he was, he was constantly anxious to be let out. If the door was opened, he would rush up to the car and sit beside it; but once he was in the car, quite uncharacteristically he still refused to settle down unless I was with him. He was, I could see, as clearly as he possibly could, day after day saying that we should go home.

It was only later that I recognised why. The start of this change in behaviour coincided with the exact time when my health had begun to deteriorate. He was trying, over and over again, to tell me that this environment was no longer doing us any good. What I could not see for myself, Bobbin, with his finely tuned sensitivity, had already perceived. He had been doing all that he could to warn me, and I was too dumb to understand.

Since that time, I have become acutely aware of my inability to conceal my ups and downs from Bobbin. Sometimes I am not sure which of us has felt 'down' first. But on those days when I feel that things seem to be more irritating or wearisome than rosy, then Bobbin, too, seems to be lacklustre and disinclined for activity. Occasionally, when some small problem is momentarily occupying my thoughts, Bobbin begins to chew his paws, and in a real crisis he has sometimes chewed them till they are raw and painful: the words of that vet the other evening rang very true.

But not all of his capacity for understanding is such a source of anxiety. Much of it is purely fascinating to contemplate. When it comes to travelling in the car, although from his position lying on the seat he cannot generally see out of the window, Bobbin always seems to know where we are and where we are going.

The first revelation of this was on our trips to the West Country. As my parents live in rural Dorset, Bobbin has enjoyed his regular visits to their village since he was eight weeks old. But he had not been there more than once or twice when I noticed that, however soundly he may have been sleeping for the first hundred miles, as soon as we got to within a mile or two of their house, he would suddenly sit up, and perch on the edge of the seat, peering out of the window and sniffing the air in evident anticipation.

Similarly, from his earliest days we have had many happy holidays staying in Devon with our friend Pauline, who had provided such excellent training with the sheep. Pauline lives in a peaceful farmhouse in a little village five miles into the hills behind Axminster. It is easy to understand that as we embark on the tortuous journey through these winding lanes Bobbin remembers where he is going. He sits up, and raising his nostrils to catch all sorts of mysterious clues from the in-flow of air through the window, he is the picture of eager expectation. If he hears the name "Tara", his favourite black Labrador friend, his paws are up on the dashboard, and he is almost unable to sit still.

What is less explicable is that, if our journey involves passing five miles on the *other* side of Axminster, with no intention of visiting Pauline, he still starts to sit up and sniff the air when we are within a few miles of the town, and continues to look hopeful until we have left it far behind. He looks so eager that sometimes, when our intended destination had been somewhere else entirely, we have turned back, and fitted in a detour to avoid disappointing Bobbin.

It is the same with all our journeys. He has a long memory. And it is no hard thing to guess, from the degree of his excitement, how happy are his memories of the place we are visiting. Once, in Wiltshire, we had the chance to call on a friend whom we had not seen for a decade. Bobbin had certainly been there only once before, and that when he was only two years old. But to my astonishment, as soon as we turned into Kitty's road, he sat up and gave unmistakable signs of recognition. For all I know, he may have been wanting to go back there for years. Perhaps he had some unfinished business in the stables with a mouse that he was still hoping to surprise.

In addition to his mastery of understanding the unspoken, there are times when it appears that Bobbin has literally understood every word that is said to him. For some months now he has been growing intermittently more deaf. I say intermittently, because there are some days on which he seems to hear far more than on others; and it is very hard to be sure exactly when he can hear and when he can't. Although this loss of hearing has some advantages - such as greater security from the alarms of fireworks - it makes me sad that one of his faculties is diminishing. In the past, he would always hear anyone who came near the house, and if any stranger came to the door he did full watch-dog duty.

Like any other self-respecting dog, he had a particular aversion to the presumption of the postman in habitually dumping things through our letter box: an intolerable liberty. For several weeks, he had appeared to be completely unaware of the daily visits of his foe. He no longer troubled to leap from his bed and bark menacingly, and it seemed to me a kind of loss that my letters were no longer perforated by tooth marks. So first thing in the morning, I took him on one side and, looking him solemnly in the eye, I said to him, "Bobbin, when the postman comes today, I'd like you to let me know. Please bark when the postman comes to our door."

You can guess the rest. An hour or so later, while I was in the kitchen, no doubt preparing a chicken casserole, suddenly Bobbin leapt off his bed with a furious burst of barking. Then he trotted straight through to the kitchen and looked at me as if to say, "Well? Was that what you wanted? Your letters are on the mat - with tooth marks."

Of course it may have been coincidence. There have been a lot of coincidences over the years. One Saturday night, after we had settled down for the evening, the phone rang at about nine o'clock. It was our friend Sue. At once it was obvious that she was upset, and within a few minutes it transpired that one of her Jack Russells had had an accident. It didn't seem to be serious, but she wanted a second opinion.
"Can I bring him over now?" she asked, "I'm not sure whether to take him to the vet."

The only problem with this was Bobbin, who was recovering from one of his flea-attacks and had at last fallen into a deep and restful sleep. Although William was one of his best friends, he would not relish being disturbed in the middle of this time of peace and relaxation. Waking him gently, I began to tell him about William's accident. "Sue is going to bring William and Annie over here now," I said. "They'll be here in about ten minutes. I'm sure he will be all right, but we must see if there's anything we can do to help."

Then I carried on watching the news, waiting to hear the sound of Sue's car.

But Bobbin was by the front door. At first he stood and looked at it, ears raised, as if he expected it to open at any moment. Then after a few minutes he lay down beside it, still clearly alert. Every now and then he came back and looked up at me questioningly, as though to say, "Well? What's keeping them? I thought you said they were coming over now." After he had been waiting for about twenty minutes, the phone rang again. William had settled down, and Sue thought it best not to disturb him. This was good news - except that now I had to explain the change of plan to Bobbin.

One of the most memorable instances of his capacity for understanding complex information occurred one warm July day when a young cousin was getting married. We were driving up to Oxfordshire with my parents, and had estimated the journey would take about three hours. It took far longer: the traffic everywhere was congested, and although we repeatedly scanned the maps for one short cut after another, it became increasingly clear that we would only just get there in time. This would be hard on Bobbin - he is always quick to get out and explore after any journey, and after so long in the car he would obviously need a break as soon as possible. There was certainly going to be no time for a walk.

I decided to explain the situation to him. After all, the ceremony would only last about twenty minutes, and then he could take priority.
"Bobbin," I said quietly, "We are going to a wedding, and we're very late. When we get there, you will have to stay in the car: you mustn't get out when we stop. You will have to wait for a little while, and then I will take you for a walk."

He looked at me with that expression of intelligence that shows that he knows he is being told something really important. He put his head on one side, cocked his ears, gazed deeply into my eyes and gave every appearance of listening carefully and trying to understand. But to be on the safe side, I repeated his instructions several times as we went along, until at last, at one minute to twelve, we arrived at the church and started looking for a place to park.

I don't think it could be said that I underestimate Bobbin's powers of comprehension, but sometimes he takes even me by surprise. As we slowed down to greet the ushers at the lych gate, and pulled into a gap in the car park, to my amazement he made no attempt to get up and see what was going on. He must have realised that we had reached our destination; he must have been interested in all the activity going on outside, as we greeted other late arrivals. But instead of sitting up expectantly to see where we were and who we were going to meet, he looked me straight in the eye, and then quietly put his head down again. Even when we scrabbled around for hats and bags, or when the doors were open as we did last minute shoe changes, he made no attempt to get up. He continued to look at me as if to say, "Don't worry: I got the message. You can rely on me," and then settled himself more comfortably on the seat and went back to sleep.

When we returned about twenty minutes later, he couldn't wait to get out. He knew that this was his time - and I think he found the scraps of smoked salmon and roast beef from the wedding breakfast sufficient compensation for any hardship he had suffered.

Chapter 19: Growing Older

It is over fourteen years now since my friendship with Bobbin began: fourteen and a half years of drawing ever closer, of understanding each other better, and occasionally, as with all friends, of misunderstandings or disagreements. We have been together more hours than we have been apart; we have explored many new places together, we have made many new friends. Together we have known some of the greatest joys that life can offer, and together we have endured times of the deepest sorrow. We have shared countless days of fun, of adventure, of excitement, of happiness and of sadness: and now we share the experience of growing older.

I certainly don't any longer have the tireless energy that I had in my youth; and Bobbin too has changed over the years. For a long time the changing was almost imperceptible. Recently, however, the signs of age have become more evident. Some days are very good, and some not so good; we take each day as it comes, and, most importantly, try to make the most of it.

To watch his gradual slowing down is at times a source of very great sadness. No more shall we go galloping over the downs with all the day ahead of us; no longer can we plan a walk that takes us over fields and heaths for as long as we please. Even though I can carry Bobbin up the hills if he seems to be out of breath, and although he can have as many rests as he chooses, I have to recognise that his interests have changed. Our days of long, adventurous walks are over.

Our outings now are far more sedate. In our younger days, Bobbin liked best to find a new place to explore: the chance to discover a new territory full of scents and adventures, to cover as much ground as possible - and to leave his mark on it. Like all of us in our youth, he sought novelty, and the intrigue of new challenges. Nowadays, what he loves best is to revisit his old familiar haunts, day after day, and to check on what has been happening there. Perhaps he feels more confident when he can predict how long our walk may be; perhaps this search for continuity gives him a deeper sense of security.

But I have discovered, too, that this change does not bring only loss: this time has also brought its own special richness and rewards. Tutored by Bobbin, I too am learning to find pleasures at a different pace. Where once a walk of less than two or three miles just did not count as a walk at all, our outings now have become mere leisurely dawdles. A walk of only half a mile may take us an hour to complete, but our enjoyment of it is perhaps even more intense than when we could cover three times the distance.

In every respect our walks are now quite different. For Bobbin, it is the secret world unlocked by his sense of smell which now absorbs almost all his attention. His quest to follow the invisible maze of messages left by fellow creatures has become ever more compelling. Every plant and post is examined with punctilious care. Quite frequently he will devote five minutes or more to the detailed, and obviously engrossing, investigation from every possible angle of a clump of nettles. For Bobbin, now, the meticulous scrutiny of scents in a small area has become more urgent than following a longer trail.

Sometimes our 'walk' takes us no further than the car park on the heath: for Bobbin, the car park is a treasure trove of fascinating smells. Here there is important work to do, finding out about who has been here since his last visit. Nose down, sensors at work, he sedulously explores these arcane mysteries, and as he wanders slowly round, he is so manifestly transported into a private world of imagination that I cannot bear to disturb him. It can take a long time thoroughly to check out all the posts around the parking area; but if Bobbin enjoys his outing, then so do I.

The other need which dominates Bobbin's walks is an increasing delight in meeting other dogs. He has always been sociable and good-natured, but now he watches out for other dogs with a new sense of urgency, as though he were making up for lost time. It is as if he feels that too much of his life has been spent with humans, and he wants to redress the balance while he can. I try to arrange his walks to offer the maximum chance of such encounters; but if we finish our excursion without having met another dog, he simply refuses to get in the car. Instead, he sits down a little distance away, alert and expectant, patiently watching for a friend to come along.

As so often in the past, I am struck by the similarity between the canine and the human. Do not many of us, as we suddenly realise that so much time has already slipped by, only in later life begin to turn our thoughts to achieving those things we did not have time for in our youth? How many of us, too, as our strength begins to wane, at last have done with great adventures, and are content instead to find comfort in the safe and familiar.

Three or four times a day we set off on our explorations. Bobbin tells me when he wants to go; and I have become quite practiced at guessing where he would like to go, too. Sometimes I get it wrong, and when we get to the field by the river, he looks at me intently and declines to get out of the car. So off we go to the common, and he leaps out at once, eager to get to work on unravelling the story of the scents.

No longer are the pace and distance of a walk always dictated by me, and I have learned to find greater pleasure in watching Bobbin's way of doing things than ever I found in making him follow mine. It took me a while to adjust to this different perspective: at first I missed ringing the changes and exploring new places. But seeing how much happier Bobbin is when I find out what he wants to do, I too have grown to discover unexpected rewards in watching the subtle changes in a favourite spot day by day. While he explores the magic world of scent, I have more time to look around me: I have time to sketch and make notes. A dog can teach you a lot, if you are willing to learn.

And so, now, our walks have become times of deep silence and profound intimacy. We wander along, absorbed in our own worlds, as if we were attached by an invisible thread. From the first, Bobbin understood the need to stay within close range, and now that he is more hard of hearing, this is even more important to both of us. Slowly we amble along, taking our time, and pausing when we please, each of us always keenly aware of exactly where the other is.

While we are going away from our starting point, I am usually about thirty yards ahead of Bobbin. But if I come to a bend in the path, or a fork, I stop and wait for him to catch up in his own time. At every turning, we check to make sure that we both choose the same path.

Once we have started to turn back, it is Bobbin who takes the lead. Now it is his turn to wait for me. If I pause to make some notes, or look at a plant, I can be certain that he is waiting patiently thirty yards ahead along the path, looking back to make sure that I am following. It is an unspoken but perfect agreement. Every now and then, one or other of us may begin to grow impatient at having to wait; then Bobbin will lurk behind a clump of bracken, or I will dodge behind a tree. He knows I will have to go and look for him if I cannot see him, and he knows that I would never go away and leave him. However well I hide, he unerringly comes straight to the spot.

So contented are we to potter around our personal patches of well-loved countryside that Bobbin sometimes seems quite dejected if we arrange to meet a friend for a walk. He makes it clear that he doesn't feel like going for this sort of walk, and once we set off, he goes as slowly as he possibly can. His lack of enjoyment is quite transparent. It is as if he feels that this intrusion will diminish the habitual tranquillity of our time together. And in some ways he is right: for talking is a great distraction from quiet contemplation, and with my attention divided, I have less time to share in his discoveries.

In other ways, too, our lives are different now. At one time the pattern of our days was ordered largely by my commitments and by my choices, and Bobbin was obliged to come wherever I went, and whenever I decided. He had his walks and his rides, but my plans always took priority. He just had to fit in. But now my priorities have changed. Now, in his aging years, it is Bobbin who comes first. I no longer think it worthwhile to become involved in activities in which Bobbin can have no part. His time is too precious. And my first and second and third priorities are Bobbin's quality of life. All of life is about choices; and that is my choice. So I am very happy to say, "No, I'm sorry, I can't come to your dinner party .... or that weekend in Bruges."

As long as Bobbin is happy, that is all that matters. I just hope that I know how to get it right.

Our evenings at home have also altered. Bobbin has never been much in favour of the television; perhaps he finds the tensions and noise intrude on this time of peace. But it was only relatively recently that I discovered his real enthusiasm: he loves to listen to classical music.

I knew that Bobbin enjoyed piano music; he has always (oh wonderful dog!) appeared to be greatly soothed by listening to me play the piano. He loves to come and lie under my feet, right by the sounding board, as if here he could feel the vibrations and absorb every note. Sometimes, in the past, when he was bored, or anxious, he would go and sit by the piano, as if to request his favourite tune. But although I have a cupboard full of tapes, I somehow never used to think of playing them. Now the tapes are in constant use: the *Flute and Harp Concerto*, the *"Spring" Sonata*, Mozart's *Sinfonia Concertante* - each has its own special place in our lives, according to our mood, or the time of day.

Of course, as he grows less robust, there are bound to be days when he feels out of sorts; when I can tell from the way he is lying that for some reason he is not comfortable. But although I have definitely become something of an expert on Bobbin's health, it is not always possible even for me to tell whether he has a headache, or a tummy ache, or maybe he just feels tired or despondent. It is no use to try to comfort him or to pat him; such unwanted attentions would only make things worse. But I have at last found an excellent remedy. If I put on a tape of the *Moonlight Sonata*, he begins visibly to unwind, and within a few minutes will be stretched out and apparently sleeping peacefully. All his cares are forgotten; and soon he flips over on to his back and lies upside down with eyes tight shut and his paws floppily dangling in the air. He is totally content and relaxed; and then I know that I, too, can really sit back and enjoy the evening.

Our evenings are quiet and uneventful; but there are also some moments that are very special. When Bobbin is truly relaxed and all is going well, then he seeks with all his powers to confide in me secrets that I can only guess at. Just sometimes, when he is lying on his sheepskin rug on the sofa in front of the fire, when he is deeply at peace, he begins to talk to me as nearly as possible in words. Although he cannot utter distinct syllables, his tone of affection and contentment is unmistakable; and our conversation takes the form of a dialogue. The tone he adopts now is completely different from those times when he longs for our guests to go. In these quiet moments he communicates in a gentle, chirruping sing-song voice, or a muttering purr. Now there are fewer variations in pitch: soft warbles of infinite tenderness alternate with low murmurs of contentment. He speaks, then I reply, in the same or an answering tone. Sometimes his tone is one of questioning; and I hope that my whispered answers reassure him. Sometimes it is as if he were saying, "This is all right. I am so cosy and happy now."

These conversations I treasure; for this is when Bobbin is trying to bridge the barriers between man and dog, and to communicate with me in a language which he feels sure I will understand. There is no other motive now: nothing to do with visitors, or food, or walks. At these times, his desire is for communication alone, in the purest and highest form that it can take.

These are indeed precious moments. But then, as if he suddenly remembered his normal habit of aloofness, and feels he has had enough of trying to speak my language, his persuasive murmurs of affection turn to expressions of brisk impatience, and the moment is at an end.

And so while our days are spent in leisurely rambles in the open air, our evenings are times of peaceful companionship. Mozart plays quietly in the background to soothe us, while Bobbin dreams and murmurs on the sofa.

I am glad that I have discovered Bobbin's preference in entertainment, while he is still able to hear well enough to enjoy his music. Perhaps it means that more and more often I have to turn off the television and miss some riveting drama because Bobbin is looking at me disapprovingly. But is that such a great hardship? It would indeed be pointlessly selfish to keep the television on when the music is a pleasure we can both enjoy.

And also a little bird once told me that Mozart is better for the soul than watching *L.A. Law*. I don't know if that is so; but I do know which Bobbin prefers.

Chapter 20: The Very Best Friend Of All

The most touching and, at times, unbearably poignant change as he grows older is a completely new and sometimes almost heart-breaking insecurity. Bobbin has always been an obliging and courteous Jack Russell, but one who shunned any unnecessary intimacy with humans. Apart from requiring certain dues, such as rides in the car and regular, suitably tasty meals, he has always been independent, at times scarcely seeming to feel the need for human company at all. Now, perhaps because his sense of hearing is not such a reliable informant as it used to be, he prefers to keep me in sight as far as possible at all times. If I am working in my study, and go out for a moment to fetch a drink of water, he is there beside me. Even when he appears to be sound asleep, he knows if I have left the room, and wherever I have gone, there he is too, within a few minutes, quietly by my feet. If he is anxious about what I may be planning, I feel a gentle touch of his damp nose on my ankle, as if for reassurance. But if he cannot track me down, he shows his anxiety by scraping up one of the woollen rugs into a comforting nest, in which he curls up, small and sorrowful, until my return. It is as if he thinks, "Now she's left me, I'll just have to do what I can for myself..."

But even now, when his powers are inevitably failing, the relationship is far from being one-sided. Bobbin can still give me useful information which I would be powerless to discover for myself. Whenever we return from one of our expeditions, as soon as he enters the front gate his nose is to the ground, and if there is any change since we went out, he sniffs carefully all the way up the path to the front door. Who has been here while we were out? Usually I soon find out; on the mat when I open the door is an envelope from Save the Children, or the free newspaper. But there are still times when the caller has left no clues for me, and only Bobbin knows who they were - he knew the moment we entered the gate.

Recently, as we were walking at dusk on a lonely common, a car suddenly drew up on the grass nearby, and a few minutes later I realised that we were being followed into the woods by a shifty-looking man in a dark suit. There was no easy way out; we were on our own, and I cursed myself for not taking more care. Bobbin had been out of sight among the long grasses, but at once he came to the rescue. Dodging my attempts to put him on the lead, instead he did something he had never done before. He rushed straight up to the stranger, and got behind him. Moving in close to his ankles, he dogged his heels with grim determination, until we were able to make our way back to the road, within reach of safety. Bobbin, with his infallible instinct and timely intervention, had once again saved me from a tricky situation.

Bobbin's deep instinct to protect his friends has not diminished. In our intimate, leisurely rambles around the countryside, Bobbin will still bark to see off a herd of cattle that charges up to the fence as we pass their field, although I would never now risk letting him try to chase them off as he so often did in his youth. And when, as we often do, we sit down on a grassy knoll or a fallen tree to enjoy a few moments' quietness during our walk, Bobbin always sits with his back to my back, careful to ensure that we are protected from intruders by being able to see in both directions.

If another dog positions himself between me and Bobbin, he growls a low and threatening growl and, as in the past, if any creature comes too close, and I say, "See him off!" Bobbin's hackles rise and he rushes to reinforce the injunction with a furious bark. He is still my protector, as much as I am his.

His deafness saddens me. For basic communications, he has learnt to follow a sign language which we have developed gradually over the last few months. But I wonder sometimes, when we are at home, whether he thinks that I don't talk to him any more. Unless I am right beside him, it is hard to know when he can hear me. It is very difficult to talk in a loud voice, and at the same time gently.

But there are still times, if the weather is cooler, when Bobbin finds the energy to race with shining eyes for the sheer joy of it, down a hill or across a grassy field: to race with head and tail held high as if he were planning to break a record. There are still times, rare and precious, when he leaps and bounds in the air for joy at greeting a favourite friend. And there are still those long, peaceful, intimate evenings when he lies stretched on the sofa beside me, his toes twitching in a glorious dream of rabbits; and times when he wakes and stretches, and gazes at me with an expression of pure contentment.

Still, if we go up to the stable or visit a friend on a farm, memories of the excitements of his youth return to him. Eagerly he scours the hedgerows for traces of rabbits; assiduously he sniffs out every trace of a mouse in the barn, and rolls in ecstasy in the straw. And if we are out at dusk, he still watches, taut in every muscle, for the coming of the fox.

Now that he is physically less vigorous, one of his chief delights is to visit his friends: he loves to explore different houses, and sometimes will even go up to a strange front door, in the hope of being invited in. He can still, like the Kosset cat, unerringly pick out the best quality carpet in the room to lie on. And when he is at home, his joy is now as it always has been, to follow the sunbeams round the house, stretching out luxuriously wherever he can find a patch of sunlight. He still finds time for taking turns to sleep in each of his many beds and favourite places. He will only at last get into his proper bed at night when each of the others has had its due turn. He is not demanding in his pleasures; but those he has, he enjoys to the full.

Bobbin is still enjoying life, and still immeasurably enriching mine. It would be impossible to count how many blessings, over our share of years, my friend has brought me. Loyalty, love and protection; an insight into joys I would never have glimpsed without him; friends he has won for us both, and beautiful places I would not have discovered alone. From Bobbin I have learnt what I could never have known without him. I have learnt to know myself better, to recognise when I am tense, or tired, or too preoccupied with trivia to give time to the important things in life. I have learnt how to enjoy what is here now to be enjoyed, to live life in the present moment and to set aside those things which are not of real importance. I have learnt that it does not matter if you cannot walk far; wherever you are, if you open your eyes, there is still much to enjoy. And I have learnt that it does not matter if there are white hairs on your suit. What matters is your smile, and cheerfulness of heart.

Each day now is a precious gift. We none of us know how many more times we may be fortunate enough to draw the curtains on another day of blessings, or on another night of peace. As long as Bobbin delights in rolling on a bale of straw, or races for sheerest joy down the grassy slope, then that day has been worthwhile, and I the luckiest of all mortals. We may not roam the hills as once we did, but we still have more than our share of joys. Life is as it should be: no more, no less. If the weather is cool, then we rejoice and set off for a walk over the heath. If it is hot, we stay at home and idle in the shade. If we are in need of a change, we have many beloved friends to visit. Whatever we do, we are free to make the best of it. And the best of it all, as far as I have discovered, is having the best of all friends to share the joys that are there and waiting, for those who are able to find them.

I would have a long search to find a friend as good as Bobbin; and I hope that he knows, among all the many things he has come to understand, what I mean when I tuck him up at night, and quietly say, "Thank you, Bobbin."

For Love of a Dog

The End